"With everything as a world, we have experienced over the last few years Kamran's new inspiring book explains how to work with the mind and our thoughts in an easy and practical way."

Kelly Hoppen CBE. Interior Designer. Author. Entrepreneur.

"Kamran explains how to work with the mind and our thoughts in a very practical and inspiring way. This book will help so many people who experience anxiety which can often feel like a lonely and confusing place. Through the guidance and exploration of the *Anxiety Antidote* it feels good to know that help is at hand."

Katie Piper OBE. Author, TV Presenter, Activist and founder of the Katie Piper Foundation.

"I worked with Kamran on an arena tour in his life as a dancer. Anxiety is what people are dealing with every day and seeing him take his current career to a new world stage where he is educating and inspiring generations of their mind, emotions and anxiety is heart-warming."

Dame Arlene Phillips DBE. Choreographer. Theatre Director and TV presenter.

"This is a book everyone should read to learn how to manage their thoughts and mental health"

Emma Mumford bestselling author of *Positively Wealthy*

This book is dedicated to the memory of my mother, for her love lives on inside of me every single second of every day.

THE
ANXIETY
ANTIDOTE

HOW AWARENESS AND ACTION CAN LEAD TO SELF-CONTROL AND INNER PEACE

KAMRAN BEDI

WATKINS
Sharing Wisdom Since 1893

This edition first published in the UK and USA in 2022 by
Watkins, an imprint of Watkins Media Limited
Unit 11, Shepperton House
89-93 Shepperton Road
London
N1 3DF

enquiries@watkinspublishing.com

1 2 3 4 5 6 7 8 9 10

Designed by Alice Coleman

Typeset by JCS Publishing Services Ltd

Printed and bound in the United Kingdom by TJ Books Ltd

A CIP record for this book is available from the British Library

ISBN: 978-1-78678-693-7 (Paperback)
ISBN: 978-1-78678-694-4 (eBook)

www.watkinspublishing.com

CONTENTS

GENERAL GUIDELINES

1. TAKING OTHER MEDICATIONS

The Anxiety Antidote **is not** a replacement for any medication that you may currently be taking. Please continue to take the diagnosed quantity of any medication that you have been prescribed by a medical professional. Always seek professional medical advice if you are considering changing, reducing and even stopping your medication intake.

2. HOW TO TAKE THE ANXIETY ANTIDOTE

Large doses of patience may be required. An open mind is also considered valuable to fully receive the benefits of the Anxiety Antidote. A daily practice of utilizing the tools and techniques will benefit you immensely. It is hugely important that you notice and embrace any positive changes that you experience, and that you share this with others.

3. POSSIBLE SIDE EFFECTS

Inner peace. Self-awareness. The sudden disappearance of anxiety. Happiness. A sense of calm and possibly more emotional self-control. Joy. The disappearance of an anxious inner voice. Suddenly asking yourself, "Why wasn't I taught this at school?", leading to possible anger (which is a different emotion to anxiety, so appreciate the change). The need and uncontrollable desire to buy multiple copies of *The Anxiety Antidote* to share with others, including strangers on the street.

Any positive side effects should be communicated on Instagram @coachkamranbedi and across all of your social media platforms using #theanxietyantidote

4. HOW TO STORE YOUR ANXIETY ANTIDOTE

Keep in reach of all children, teenagers and adults. Ensure it is fully visible and displayed to generate interest from others so that it may improve the mental health and anxiety symptoms of other humans on earth. Recommended for display on all commuter journeys, including trains, buses, subways, planes, boats, submarines and all other public spaces.

A NEW DAY DAWNS

Kamran: When you think about your anxiety, what do you hear inside your mind? What is your inner voice saying? Just take a moment and connect with it; hear it, let it speak.

Client: It is generally considering "what if" situations, like "What if I say something stupid and everyone laughs at me?" or "What if I get stuck on the train and can't get off?"

Kamran: Thank you. And with what you hear, what do you see in the space of your thoughts? As you think and hear this inner dialogue, are there any pictures?

Client: Sometimes.

Kamran: Close your eyes if it helps and access the sounds and pictures. What do you see?

Client: I see the worst happening. People laughing at me, or me panicking on the train, feeling stuck… and it ends there in my mind.

Kamran: And what do you feel from what you see and what you hear?

Client: Anxious.

Kamran: And where are those anxious feelings located in your body? Take a moment to connect with them and feel where they are now.

Client: In my stomach.

Kamran: Describe the shape to me of the anxious feelings that are in your stomach and if there is any movement.

Client: It's like a round knot that's moving around as though it's in a washing machine. I sometimes wake up and this feeling in my stomach is already there.

Kamran: OK, I am going to show you how to work with your anxious inner voice, how to stop the anxious thoughts that you see in your mind and how to ease the feelings in your stomach quickly.

Client: If I knew how to do that, I would feel so much better... I'd feel like the old me.

Kamran: Then let me show you how.

THE APPROACH

As an anxiety and mindset practitioner, one of the most common things I hear from my clients who are experiencing anxiety is, "I just want to feel like the old me." This theme comes up session after session, week after week, just as in the above conversation.

Another common question that I am asked is: "How did you know that I have the voice in there?" I have explored this further with various individuals who have even gone on to say, "I thought it was only me that had that anxious inner chatter," or "I didn't realize that people talk so much inside their head."

"**We all do it**" is usually my answer, because it's true. We all think through pictures and have internal sounds. Most people, however, do not listen to that inner monologue or take notice of the pictures going through their minds; they just let them happen.

If you want to change or improve something in your life, including your anxiety, you must first begin to change and improve the thoughts that are being formed in your mind. These thoughts have a very real effect on how you feel and, consequently, behave.

I'm sure you would have benefited greatly in your life if you had been taught at school how to understand **how** you are thinking, **what** it is making you feel, behave and experience, and **how** to effectively change your thoughts to improve how you are feeling. This is not something many of us are shown how to do. Whether you are 14 years old or 80 years old, learning about your mind and how to work with your thoughts can and will allow you to have a better experience in "operating" your mind and your emotions.

You may currently have some or even no awareness of your thoughts or how to work with them, and know how to use your smartphone better than you know how to use your mind. The good news, however, is that you can learn this and I am going to guide you through it.

NEURO-LINGUISTIC PROGRAMMING

My coaching, and the methods contained in this book, centre around the principles of Neuro-Linguistic Programming (NLP), which is based on the idea that the mind directly influences the body. So, to begin, let's dive a little deeper into NLP.

NLP allows you to understand the structure of your thoughts and identify the specific thoughts that are causing you to think, feel and behave in a particular way. Once this is understood, you will be able to explore, edit, improve or even suggest new thought patterns to achieve your desired outcome.

"Neuro" relates to our senses and how we take in our personal experiences from what we see, hear, feel, and even smell and taste through each moment of each experience. The elements of our senses are then translated into the "linguistics" which is the "language of the mind". These are the thoughts that we think and the words and language that we use to communicate inside our head about situations and experiences in our lives. The "programming" looks at the patterns that we run with our thinking that then influence our behaviour and the results that we have in our life. It might help to think of NLP as the "instructions manual" of your mind! Once we know and understand the language, we can work to change the result.

As an example, an individual may walk down the street, see a dog walking towards them (neuro), hear a voice in their head through their thoughts that says something like, "that dog looks scary" (linguistic), which leads them to feel fear, or panic and therefore they cross the road (programme) to avoid any close proximity to the dog.

An anxiety-related example would be an individual thinking about a social event that is happening later that day and imagining, through the pictures in their mind, all of the ways that it could go wrong (neuro). They may then hear their inner voice through their thoughts, from the pictures they see in their mind, repeatedly saying, "Tonight is going to be a disaster" (linguistic), which leaves them feeling tight and tense in their body and as a result, they decide not to go (programme).

For the NLP approach to be successful, it is important to really understand the person's subjective experience of their situation. In my coaching, I tend to delve deep into "how" they are thinking to identify "what" their thoughts are, and "how" those thoughts then cause them to feel and behave. I ask directed questions to really hone in on this, as in the conversation that began this chapter. Once I know all of this, I can find the best way to treat them by introducing the appropriate interventions, tools and resources that will allow them to have more control over their thoughts, which will ultimately lead to less anxiety, more self-control and more inner peace.

WHAT IS THE ANXIETY ANTIDOTE?

In this book, I will be sharing my approach and adapting it so that you can follow it easily at home. I want you to think of this book in its entirety as your own personal Anxiety Antidote: something for you to turn to when you need it, and also to prepare you to resist and overcome anxiety in the future. The book, and how you use it, will be individual to your situation, your experiences and your needs, so you will be the alchemist of your antidote, so to speak! I have seen these techniques used effectively for many years by clients who have taken the specific work that was set for them and actively used it as and where needed.

There are three sections to the Anxiety Antidote:

1. **Self-Awareness**
2. **Self-Action**
3. **New Self**

The first section of the book, "**Self-Awareness**", functions as the in-depth personal consultation and exploration of the individual subjective experience of anxiety that I would normally begin with in early coaching sessions.

In this section, I will help you develop an increased sense of awareness of your own mindset, the structure of your thoughts, the type of thinker you are, your personal anxiety symptoms, any anxiety patterns and your focus for this book. I will teach you how to become more self-aware of the present moment, allowing you to actively shift your focus away from any overthinking or spiralling thoughts, which is going to be a skill that you can use for the rest of your life. It will also provide an in-depth look at the specific symptoms of anxiety, the mental and physical patterns of anxiety, and the mind–body connection.

The "**Self-Action**" part of the book is full of methods, tools and techniques which you can use at any time and in any place to help you improve the way that you are thinking and feeling.

The final section, "**New Self**", looks to the future and guides you in ways to integrate all of your learnings and the tools on offer into your day-to-day life.

HOW TO USE THIS BOOK

I suggest that you work your way slowly and carefully through each section, as the Anxiety Antidote works in the same way that my coaching sessions do: it takes you on a curated journey that has been designed to help you work with your anxiety.

A GP would prescribe a course of antibiotics to be taken for a number of days from start to finish. Missing days or not finishing the course of antibiotics would most likely not result in the outcome that you hoped for. Also, by going through the book from start to finish, you can avoid missing any bits that will be a vital ingredient for your own personal antidote!

From experience, the importance of formulating habitual patterns of thinking that work for you is greatly encouraged to work on your mind on a daily basis. This will strengthen your ability to think in ways that allow you to change and improve how you feel, quickly. If you think about learning how to drive a car or ride a bike, you generally learn specific steps, an order to start the movement like check your mirrors, put the key in the ignition, make sure the car is in neutral and then you start the car. The specific steps become an unconscious habit where you don't consciously think about what you are having to do, as driving a car quite quickly becomes habitual. From a very young age, learning to walk, write and read, playing an instrument, learning a subject and operating any piece of equipment will have required **learning**, **practice** and **repetition**. I ask you to approach the Anxiety Antidote in the same way, applying it as often as required, but also each and every day as a preventative measure, until it comes to you more naturally.

From consultation, exploration, intervention, to self-accountability, in person or through this book, it is through your own self-accountability that you utilize the methods that work for you to best experience the results in your life. Use this opportunity to increase your self-knowledge, self-awareness and the open possibilities of a new-found self-control.

THE A WORD

What is certain in an uncertain world? **Anxiety**.

Perhaps you've been ready for times of uncertainty from months or even years of knowing what it feels like to live inside your own skin, anticipating the worst-possible outcomes that captivate your mind and emotions?

This is what living on the edge is like.

Anxiety comes in waves, often tsunamis of weight that force you to withdraw from the world around you. As you dissociate into the narrative that's screaming around inside your head, your anxiety shows up. Your emotions may often feel like you've bungee-jumped into the unknown, where you believe the rope is going to snap. Yet here you are still bobbing along, being dipped into various depths of gut-churning drops, each and every day.

Fight, flight or freeze?

All of them.

Fighting yourself, freezing from life and flying at an altitude with catastrophic turbulence.

Another day, another episode.

A different day, an anxiety attack.

Is there any peace from the tornado of thoughts that plagues your body with these endless emotions?

Take the Antidote.

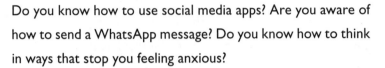

A LIGHT BULB MOMENT
FOR MENTAL HEALTH

Do you know how to use social media apps? Are you aware of how to send a WhatsApp message? Do you know how to think in ways that stop you feeling anxious?

I'm guessing that you answered yes to the first two questions, and no to the third. This is the general response I've had from asking individuals and audiences, to gain a better understanding of what people can do well and with ease. Dealing with anxiety and generally improving one's mental health, seems to be the area that people do not know "how to do". I first had this collective, enlightening realization when I asked a live audience at the Mind Body Spirit Festival in London.

It was spring of 2019 and I was delivering a talk on dealing with daily mental health challenges including anxiety, depression, stress and "how to cope". As the event featured crystal healing, shamanism, chanting to CBD oils, I felt there was a possible gap in the line-up and an opportunity for me to cover areas around mental health. My proposal for my talk was accepted and I was added to the live stage line-up. I wasn't surprised that the auditorium was full when I arrived. With talks on "communicating with angels" to "manifesting miracles", I seemed to be a needle of mental health advice in a haystack of alternative therapies.

With a couple of hundred people sat waiting for me to start, I mentally went through my notes on what to offer this audience in this space at this time. I felt comfortable, at home and at ease ready to take the stage. As people chatted to one another, others glared at their phones, scrolling, taking selfies keeping the time passing by. There were people of all ages, men and women, as well as a handful of kids who I assume had been taken for the day to explore the world of the Mind Body Spirit Festival. It was time for me to start. I walked up the three steps and on to the small stage. Mic in hand, audience still in their own worlds, my aim was to hook everyone's attention. You may think it's quite plain sailing, you're on stage, the audience is there to listen, but I wanted them to more than listen. I wanted them to understand, to search within themselves from what I had to share. I decided to introduce myself and immediately ask three simple questions. This was my chance to get the audience on board, to participate and for me to really be heard.

"Thank you for joining me on this lovely spring afternoon," I said as I glanced across the room as people's eyes, attention and awareness lifted to my direction. "My name is Kamran Bedi, I am a mental health practitioner who works with people around their anxieties and also post-traumatic stress disorder." Big picture and short intro, I was then into my possible hook. "I would like to start by asking you all collectively a few simple questions". More people entered, with a small crowd now standing at the door and also behind the back row. "If you could raise your hand as you answer so I can get a full idea of where you may personally be in response to my questions, I can then share with you the best of my professional knowledge with the aim to educate and inspire you here today."

Question one. "OK, please consider: 'Who here knows how to work a mobile phone?' Please raise your arm up nice and high so that I can see if yes, you know how to work a mobile phone." The entire room raised an arm. "Excellent, thank you." Question two. "Please keep your arm raised in the air if you know how to use Facebook or Instagram." Pretty much the room remained the same, with arms still up as I glanced around the room. It felt as though everyone was on board, they were with me, participating and following my introduction and questions, and then the energy of the room suddenly changed. Final question. "Please keep your arm raised in the air if you know how to use your mind." Like a collective of lead balloons the sea of arms and faces in front of me dropped down faster than you could say *anxiety*. People's eyes dropped down towards the floor. There were expressions of confusion. A few people glanced around to see the result and there I felt it, the reality right in front me, people of all ages, all different types of education, cultures and life experiences, but the collective answer of "No, I do not know how to use my mind."

Now it's a pretty ambiguous question which can and does have a variety of ways that it could be answered, so I went on by finally being a bit more specific. "When I say use your mind, what I mean specifically is, do you know how to stop yourself feeling anxious, stressed, depressed or emotionally low, through your thoughts?" I had a few half-raised "yes" responses and I continued into my talk.

As a professional practitioner, I often hear people open up about their specific and difficult experiences with anxiety and even post-traumatic stress disorder. I hear people also talking about sometimes having a lack of confidence, low self-worth and a collection of experiences that has left them feeling as though they can't move forward in their lives. So many people seem to live on edge, in fear or often spend endless time overthinking the worst possible scenarios that could happen, which leaves them feeling anxious. I also see repetitive patterns from person to person, where there's a struggle to deal with the thoughts and anxious emotions that live and play out within.

It was in my live realization on stage, and I have re-lived it asking the same questions to different audiences, that we as a nation know how to use social media apps, our phones, our messaging and communication devices, yet we struggle with operating and understanding our own minds. In my professional opinion, one of the main difficulties that people face with their anxiety is explaining in detail or even just in a small number of words, how they are feeling on the inside. I guess, in general, people tend to struggle when opening up about their feelings in great detail. Whether it's friends, colleagues, family or even myself, the umbrella terms of "I'm feeling good", "I could be better" or "I have anxiety" are where most people start, if they even start. Not only is it difficult to explain in words, let alone specific detail, of the pain and strife you may feel within, the concept of understanding, looking at and even possibly then communicating how your mind works and operates can be as confusing as experiencing anxiety.

How do you describe the feeling of being on edge so that others understand that your life feels like this pretty much all of the time? The constant feelings of being unmotivated, lethargic and emotionally low can also feel like a struggle to put into a few simple sentences or even for you to personally understand. I know this all too well personally and professionally, that it really can feel quite overwhelming. One of the main aims of me writing this book is to give you a clear understanding of what your anxiety is, how it is formed and different ways for you to deal with it.

From a scientific standpoint, anxiety begins in the mind with your thoughts which then influences the autonomic nervous system. There are two essential aspects to your autonomic nervous system: the sympathetic system and the parasympathetic system. When it senses a threat, the sympathetic nervous system will distribute energy accordingly, shifting your body and brain into "fight or flight" response. The "threat" could be external, in situations and circumstances that are happening around you in your life, or internal, in the form of the thoughts that you think. No matter whether that threat is real or not, your body will respond as if it is and prepare you to either face it head on (fight) or run away from it as fast as possible (flight). (For more on the physical response to anxiety, see page 58.)

Meanwhile, the parasympathetic system helps your body to calm and centre, relax and digest, and also assists in returning to "normal". Both aspects of the autonomic nervous system should work harmoniously together, however if a person experiences too much stress, worry, negative thinking and feelings of anxiety, they may end up overly activating the sympathetic side, which can cause imbalances of the nervous system. Feeling on edge for no reason can leave you feeling physical symptoms of anxiety and can in many ways affect various aspects of your health. Struggling to sleep, feeling fatigued, experiencing digestion issues, skin conditions and changes in your mood and personality can all be experienced over time if the nervous system remains on high alert.

ABOUT ME

One of the main aims of me writing this book is to give you a clear understanding of what your anxiety is, how it is formed and different ways for you to deal with it. This in many ways comes from my professional training, experience and knowledge that I want to share with you, but also from my very early experiences of extreme personal anxiety. Whether you can communicate what you're feeling but feel as though nobody gets you, understands you or relates to you, or whether you're finding it hard to understand the overwhelm that lives inside of you, my aim is to help you. Help you to understand, to inspire you to take action, and to feel the changes that you can create for yourself from my guidance. This is because I had anxiety before I was a professional practitioner. I had experienced a lot of anxiety where I had no help but an overwhelming internal personal struggle, and I know how difficult it is to understand and deal with anxiety. Through this book, it is my aim to help you to assist you in finding and exploring various options that could cause you to feel more inner peace and more mental and emotional control.

You may be highly educated in your field or greatly experienced in the colourful lessons of life. However, I discovered a key missing piece of the jigsaw of my life in my early twenties. I can look back to those younger years and notice where I experienced my mind and my thoughts to be an entity of their own. I would at times sit and patiently watch and listen to the thoughts inside my head as if I were a tenant occupying the space and place inside my own head. I was surrounded by the uninvited company of my thoughts, where at times it would feel quite uncomfortable being in the presence of what my thoughts were thinking. Life for me back then was generally easy, and the overthinking would usually happen as I lay in bed at night. My mind was full of aspirations. I would think and dream of the life I wanted to live, the experiences that I wanted to have and then I'd fall into a peaceful sleep. It was years later where I discovered the tone and narrative about myself and life in general, which was playing out through my thoughts, had become more negative. It was beginning to get draining and inescapable, and the patterns of thoughts that I began to despise became regular and repetitive, as did the feelings they made me feel.

I quickly found relief through self-help books. Not only did I discover the various ways I could direct and change my thoughts, I also meditated daily and soon enough began to train in various disciplines around the mind and body. Self-development and self-discovery nourished me in ways that back then I didn't know were possible. Investing time in my mind and my emotions, beyond my professional training has given me a journey of over a decade of developing myself. The results came from the first exploration from NLP (Neuro-Linguistic Programming) books and YouTube guided meditations. The fruits of my labour have now allowed me to develop and share further with the people I now professionally work with.

From the one-to-one work I continue to do online and clinically, I have encountered thousands of people who have struggled with the experience of anxiety. The reality of seeing nearly two hundred people in one space and at one time answer that they did not know how to use their mind, highlighted to me the potential disastrous pandemic of difficult mental health challenges that millions of people across the world, young and old, may one day face.

From my professional and personal experience, the reality is that it can seem difficult to communicate how you are feeling on the inside. It can cause you more emotional discomfort, however it's important for me to also highlight that change and healing is available and is possible for everyone. The opportunity to learn a variety of ways that help your mind, where you can potentially find inner peace, have more self-awareness and possible control, is now something that you can experience for yourself. Having experienced the power of self-help, self-educating yourself is something that you can take part in daily, which doesn't have to take up much time. Sacrificing some of the time spent aimlessly scrolling on your smartphone is a sacrifice you can make to give time to improving your mental and emotional health, right from this very day. You do not have to suffer in silence as I did when I was younger, for you can learn to communicate silently yet powerfully within yourself through your thoughts to think and feel better. This can and will allow you to then create and experience a sense of mental and emotional ease that can lead to more possible self-control. This can change how you experience your life more positively and more freely. It is a position that you can now take for yourself where you raise your arm and declare, "I am now learning the many ways of dealing with my thoughts and emotions to help my anxiety be at ease." In shifting from being a victim of your thoughts, to instead now being a student of your own mind, you can allow your life to transform from a position of feeling limited, to now thinking and feeling ways that leave you feeling limitless.

QUESTION?

TELL ME WHAT YOU THINK ...

Do you know how to use a smartphone?

Do you know how to use Instagram or other social media apps?

Can you stop yourself feeling anxious?

Can you improve your mental and emotional state quickly?

Do you know how to use your mind?

Are you willing to learn how?

LIFE ON
THE EDGE

Towards the end of my first relationship, I was exhausted with anxiety. The feelings of uncertainty, being unsure of my future and not being in control, led me to feel and experience the most intense physical anxiety I've ever experienced. The weight of my world had come crashing down inside of me, into the physical embodiment of crippling anxiety. I could not feel any other emotion apart from the burden of my anxious world that I carried around inside of me each and every day. Even as I lay in bed at night, it felt as though a weight of water was holding me down, as my body struggled to move out of this inner body experience that anchored me into what only felt like pain. It was as if I was holding my breath and trying to live at the same time. My exterior was a fake smile, a nod here and there, where my strength went only to formulating the words to not reveal that I was on the verge of collapse. It wasn't the anxiety that I was hiding or the situation in hand, it was the knowing that no matter what anyone said, advised, offered or suggested, the feelings within just felt like nothing could bring them to ease. The description of falling back on a chair, trying to catch myself from falling over was where I was twenty-four hours of those anxious days. That grasp for air that suddenly grabs your attention as you try to find your feet. That uncertainty you feel in a panic of falling back, with the possibility of pain. That split second that could go either way. I was there full time. As my mind raced, my heart continued to break and as my body froze, the fight to continue was like walking a tightrope through life.

Perhaps you have had similar feelings, and these are physical and mental experiences that you can relate to? Whether it's regarding relationships, health or even finances, the grip of anxiety can feel hard to shake off.

I have worked with people and often hear from people who have experienced anxiety for decades. Living on edge, existing in the place and space of uncertainty in their body as a constant daily experience has been something that they have lived with for long periods of time. Perhaps this is the case for you? The stark and grave reality is how their life has been held back from avoiding working on their anxious feelings within. It is in the avoidance, through the choice of being strong, where they often carry the weight of their mental and emotional world within, that relationships get damaged, dreams get diverted or abandoned and a new uncomfortable sense of reality becomes their new normal. It is through the avoidance of dealing with or working on their anxiety where their energy becomes focused on trying to cope and hold it all together, but they end up not fully living. Avoiding the anxiety, repressing it within or ignoring it can change and shape your personality in ways that do not need to happen. Attempting to live with an emotional mental weight is as difficult as you trying to carry a 10-kilogram weight on your shoulders day in, day out. Yet people seem to continue through their life, distancing themselves from the opportunity to put the weight down, building perseverance to carry forth the burden of anxiety, fully unaware of the long-term impact it can have on other areas of their life.

You may have had anxiety for a short or long period of time, but perhaps you have noticed that it has got stronger over time in the way that you experience your anxious feelings? There may be times where your anxiety disappears out of sight and then periods where it is back and possibly more overwhelming. You may have felt confused, uncertain, frustrated and helpless. I know I did in those younger years, when I knew of no way to cope with the feelings and burden of my anxiety. From feeling confused about what I was feeling mentally and emotionally, to times where I felt out of control from an anxiety attack, any form of knowledge to stop the anxiety would have been welcomed with open arms.

Let this now be the time that you choose to follow my guidance to explore some of the ways that you can deal with your anxious thoughts and feelings. The fact that you are reading this book strongly suggests that you are looking for help, and I must stress that the power is in your hands, to activate and direct your mind and emotions to feel the freedom that is on offer. It is a journey worth exploring, for I strongly believe that the missing part of any individual's education is how to work with their own mind and emotions. This is a pattern and common problem that I have encountered professionally every week for the last 10 years. I continue to work with people who have no idea how to use their mind to manage their thoughts and anxious feelings.

You probably confidently know how to use your phone and your social media apps, and you probably gave yourself time and commitment to learning how to use them now without thinking. It's now time for you to explore the functions of your own mind, as you discover and most importantly learn, practise and embody the information for how your mind works and the methods that are on offer to help you develop more self-control over your mind, emotions and anxiety.

YOUR BODY SPEAKS
FROM WITHIN

On the outside you might appear calm or maybe even detached from the present moment. But on the inside it feels as if there is a plague of anxious emotions that you cannot escape from. Your gut is churning, your legs feel weak, like jelly ready to collapse. Then there are times that the tremors in your legs solidify into weights that feel like anchors, making each step you take feel like an effort that threatens to exhaust you completely.

Your mind resembles a lighthouse, alert, searching for any possible threat. Your eyes are wide open, and you can see so far ahead into the future that your neck is sore from carrying the weight of a "**what if**" world on your rounded shoulders. You want to curl into a ball but if you sit, you feel it. If you walk, it goes with you.

The feelings of anxiety captivate your entire body, from feeling heavy and dark, glistening with unattractive body sweats, as if you need anything more to deal with. Oh, and then there are the short breaths, the icing on the cake to make your already overwhelmed body become starved of its birthright of oxygen.

You ask yourself, will you ever feel like the old you again?

Yes.

The body keeps the score but the mind drives the body. You pull yourself back from the edge of the cliff. You are here. You are present. You are aware.

PART ONE

SELF-AWARENESS

Understanding yourself is the first step of any personal breakthrough. You can often feel confused by your emotions and powerless to stop an overactive mind, but by becoming self-aware, your personal power over the feelings of anxiety will increase, as you begin to build a bridge that makes it easier to travel over difficult emotional waters. Let's step inside and begin.

YOUR INNER
COMPASS

As you ride the rollercoaster of life, you may often feel as though you're out of control, that you cannot predict the dips and turns that lie ahead. Some days may be easy, but then you find yourself disturbing that sense of ease by thinking through a maze of complex possible scenarios in your head.

Do you get lost in the world of your mind where your thoughts are being tossed from emotion to emotion like a ship sailing through aggressive waters?

How do you navigate your way to peace, and is such a thing even possible?

The answer is YES.

FROM CONFUSION TO CLARITY

A lot of my coaching work that utilizes NLP helps me to identify what a client wants to focus on, discuss, work through and improve where necessary. From an NLP point of view, getting specific with what you are feeling when you're anxious can help you get a deeper understanding of your mind and emotions, which can lead you to take action and improve your situation. It's quite common when you're anxious to get stuck mentally, emotionally and then physically in the experience of your anxiety. You may end up lost in your thoughts, mentally drained, emotionally tense and physically exhausted. This can quickly become a pattern, whereby thoughts go round and around inside your head, feeding the uncomfortable feelings in your body.

Anxiety can feel overly confusing. I know this from my own experiences of anxiety and from the people who I work with who often find it difficult to communicate their feelings, thoughts and physical sensations.

A pattern I have seen on a regular basis over the years is that anxiety is used as an umbrella term. I rarely hear people say "I am panicking", "I feel nervous", "I am sad", "I feel emotionally low", "I am scared", "I am losing control", "I feel on edge", "I am really exhausted" – instead it has become more and more common to summarize with the word "anxious". This in itself can be quite limiting. Without getting specific about your feelings and emotions, you can end up preventing yourself from shifting and overcoming your anxiety. Consider if you were to go to the doctor and simply said, "I feel ill." Without explaining your symptoms, how can you or the doctor understand or find any solution to your problem? Similarly, if you said to a colleague at work, "There's a problem", this very vague statement would probably be met with, "What (specifically) is the problem?" Remaining vague means the cycle of anxiety can build in strength, where you are lost in the feelings but not necessarily identifying or working on the root cause. By becoming more self-aware and identifying the specific feelings that you are experiencing, you can gain a better understanding and consider the cause of them, which then allows you to consider possible solutions.

The key areas you'll explore as you progress through this work are:

- How and what specifically you are feeling
- How and what specifically you are thinking
- What specifically is happening in your life that is causing your anxiety
- How to change what you are thinking and therefore how you are feeling

Your exploration through these four areas will equip you with the understanding you need to then use any of the presented processes to change your anxiety experience for the better.

For your first area of self-reflection, consider the following:

1. **When you are anxious, what feelings specifically are you feeling?**

There may be a few feelings that blend together. By taking a moment to pause when you're anxious, you can turn your focus within and ask yourself with your inner voice, "What feelings am I specifically feeling?"

Is it sadness? Fear? Panic? Nervousness? Anger? Shame? Guilt? Hurt? Regret? Frustration? Depression? Or anything else specifically?

As you question yourself, reflect, consider and identify your feelings, you are actually shifting your thinking from anxious thoughts in order to do so. This shift in focus, in and of itself, can begin to disempower the feelings of anxiety and weaken its grip.

Having identified the specific feelings, you can now move on to the next step to break down and understand your anxiety further. Consider the following:

2. **What is causing you to feel these feelings? What is happening in your life that is specifically causing these feelings?**

Your feelings and emotions can act as a compass that directs you to the cause of your anxiety. Many individuals can identify their feelings as sadness caused by a challenge in their relationship, or stress caused by mounting pressures at work. It could be fear in relation to a health issue or frustration in a friendship. These feelings and emotions that are identified are not anxiety. They are specific feelings that have a specific cause. Sometimes the cause may appear to be more personal in relation to how you're thinking and not so external as a particular life situation; it may be a series of thought patterns that you need to address that are running riot in your mind. The methods I'm going to share with you in the "Self-Action" section will help you to deal with your mindset and your thoughts; however, in your self-reflection for when you are anxious, you may discover that there is an external situation that, once addressed or dealt with, your anxiety will then reduce or even disappear.

If you are able to identify the specific cause of your negative feelings, you can then consider the third step:

3. **What can I do to improve these feelings? Are there any specific actions that I need to take to reduce these feelings that are the cause of my anxiety?**

This could include communicating with other people involved, resolving personal issues, setting boundaries around the areas that are influencing your anxiety or even seeking further professional help or advice. Anything avoided, left unattended or "up in the air" can and will continue to cycle the thoughts and feelings of anxiety throughout the body, prolonging the discomfort that is felt within.

At a time when I was feeling anxious, I identified the specific feeling as panic. The cause for this was the information my builder had given me, informing me that I needed a new roof. I was experiencing panic from the suggestion of the work, the financial obligation and the time frame involved, which would affect my work schedule. I realized to improve these feelings, I needed to talk further with him, get specific on the details and get a second opinion (it turned out that the work didn't need to be done immediately). The anxiety lasted as long as I allowed myself to feel the panic. The immediate step back and realization that I needed to talk with him and get more detail interrupted the thought patterns of panic that only existed in my head, where I was catastrophizing possible worst-case scenarios. Having the conversation I knew I needed then led me to clarity, and my anxiety lifted.

Any form of self-reflection can help you shift from being in a stuck position to a more resourceful or even resolved position, and it is something that I personally wish I had known in my younger years. Having been through a lot of anxiety in my twenties where I had no idea what was happening to me as the overwhelm of the feelings left me confused, I know that it is easier said than done to find relief from it. What I also know and now champion is that peace is an option, even when you are continuing through an uncertain and unresolved period in your life. By turning your focus towards the specific cause of your anxiety, you then have the opportunity to experience immediate and long-term healing by taking action.

In my difficult days of uncertainty, the one thing I was certain of was what I could do and what I had to do to take the edge off those anxious feelings. I had to save myself and address the cause. I had to put the work into using my awareness to move past the anxiety I felt and lived through so that I could survive.

This was a daily action of working specifically on the feelings of panic, overthinking the worst, and addressing the sadness that I felt within. There were a few areas of my relationship I actively had to address, but my anxiety was mainly created from my thought patterns, which I got lost in. That was the specific experience underneath the label "anxiety". It was then a mental practice that I engaged in through my difficulties to help myself reduce the overwhelm of the anxious feelings, leading me to experience different levels of inner peace. This practice of self-reflection is all part of the antidote which you are going to apply to help you create more peace of mind in your life.

A TIME TO REFLECT –
AND HEAL

You can heal the areas of your life that feel damaged within your mental and emotional body. Do this to protect what you love in your life, as, if left unchecked, it can fester within and begin to destroy the good.

A band aid will not fix you, but *you* can fix you.
So, look inside and isolate the source of the hurt.
Find it. Work with it. Heal it and free it.

WHERE ARE YOU IN YOUR MIND?

The structure of your mind will help identify where your focus is with your thoughts. It could be the past or future you're thinking about, or present-day challenges. Examining **what** and **how** you are thinking is part of this NLP process to decode and understand the structure of your mental and emotional experience. Attention is also paid to the behaviours that a person does and the results that those behaviours produce, which will all stem from the "how" and "what" a person is thinking. Thoughts and behaviour are key in understanding, assessing and then improving any area of an individual's life, and especially so with anxiety.

A GP may offer general advice, including "try to relax", "practice mindfulness, speak to someone" or reduce any stress. From an NLP point of view, it's important and extremely helpful to look at **how** to relax, **how** to be mindful, **how** to speak about and understand your anxiety, and **how** to reduce stress. This comes from firstly discovering what it is you are doing inside your head in relation to your thoughts.

So, to start with, think about your thoughts. That is what most people fall powerless to, as they tend to not observe, listen to, or consider their thoughts. They mostly feel that their thoughts just happen to them and that they have no control or influence over the thoughts that play out inside the space of their mind. But first, ask yourself the following questions:

- What are you usually thinking when you're anxious?
- Are you thinking back to the past and then feeling anxious in the present about the future?
- Do you think more about the future and consider the worst possible outcomes, which feeds the feelings of anxiety in your body?
- How do you know your thoughts are true?

You probably have beliefs that you consider to be 100 per cent true for you in your life and in your reality. Those beliefs will be backed up by specific experiences that allow you to stand firm in them. With anxiety, most people will consider and construct various scenarios with their thinking that are not actually true. They are simply considerations of what may possibly happen in the immediate or near future, "what if"-type thoughts. They can be possible threats that could come up and worst-case scenarios that are thought over and over but are in fact presently untrue. You may even think back to the past to difficult situations, past anxious experiences which then project you into the future, imagining scenarios which cause you to feel anxious in the present moment. Most of the things that you have considered to be worst-case situations have probably never happened before. They likely only exist in your mind, but are felt in your body as fear, panic and worry, which you label as anxiety.

Beth spent so much of her time inside her head thinking "what if" after "what if" about her future. The detail that she had created and experienced in her thoughts, the pictures she saw and the scenes that she watched, left her feeling a general state of anxiety. She rarely felt present and mainly felt the anxiety that gripped her body, but upon reflection she confirmed that so much of her thinking was ahead on the worst-case scenarios.

Paul realized that he would think back to the past and consider experiences that caused him fear and panic, which then propelled his thoughts to the future for possible threats that could come. Hearing his inner voice talking freely inside his head about what had previously happened led him to feel future panic and fear, which he labelled as anxiety. He had assumed he was an anxious person and anxious in general. Through my questioning, which guided him to explore his feelings and the cause of those feelings, he realized his fear and panic was only rooted in one area from particular past experiences. He had come to believe that he was an anxious person all the time, but soon realized that so much of his future-based thinking was influenced by one specific area that he feared.

It is natural for you, through the thousands of thoughts that you have each and every day, to think back to the past and ahead to the future and to spend so much time in the space of your mind. As you shift your mind through various aspects of time you may generate a variety of feelings and emotions in your body. In gaining a deeper understanding of where your thoughts are taking you, you can then begin to break the cycle of thinking to become more mindful and more present. The key is to now become aware for **how** and **what** you are thinking.

WHAT IF?

What if you need to think about what if it happens? Or what if you need to think about what if it doesn't happen? What if you don't think about the situation that could happen? What if you lose control? What if that one day or one moment goes wrong? What if you get it right? Or what if they don't like it, or you, or how you do it, say it, present it? What if you are wrong? What if they don't think you can do it? What if you don't know what to what if?

Anxiety.

What if I understand my feelings? What if I feel in control? What if I work on my thoughts? What if I begin to feel better? What if I feel present? What if I don't hear my anxious inner voice anymore? What if I practise working with my mind? What if things get better quickly?

Antidote.

BREAKING
THE CYCLES

Repetition is the key to training the subconscious mind. To create a new pattern for your mind, I recommend repeating each method, following the steps involved and practising it a minimum of **five times**. I will remind you of this throughout the book, as the importance of repetition when it comes to dealing with anxiety cannot be overstated.

Repetition will help you to build awareness, understanding and competence. Once you have achieved competence, you can use the Anxiety Antidote methods by yourself in your own time. You can also refer back to the questions and methods in the book, as you may find they become the basis of a positive habit of self-reflection.

It's hugely important for you to **notice any positive shifts that you experience**. If you feel calmer, more relaxed, less in your own head or a general reduction in your feelings of anxiety, make sure to acknowledge the shifts that you are creating for yourself. It can be quite common to fix one thing in your life, not notice it and then fixate on another area of your life that causes you to feel anxious, so really pay attention to any shifts that you create and experience how you are feeling for the better.

FEELING PRESENT

When you're feeling anxious, there's a strong chance that you are deep inside your thoughts, thinking about the situations in your life that are then causing you to feel anxious in your body. The thoughts that you see and hear in your mind will be consuming you and pulling you out of the present moment. You could be at work, with friends or family, or sat at home on the sofa watching your thoughts play out in your mind. As you focus inside of yourself, giving time to the thoughts that play out in your own head space, the feelings of anxiety will build in your body. You will have likely mentally time-travelled ahead into the future and left your body in the space that you stand, sit or walk in, and are distracted from the present moment.

Where are you going in your mind with your thoughts when you're anxious: ahead into the future or back into the past?

Most people tend to time travel ahead and think about possible threats, worst-case scenarios, things that they fear could happen, or they are trying to mentally establish control around a situation in their life as they consider it. The most common thought pattern that is experienced when a person is feeling anxious are thoughts of "what if". The dreaded "what if" thoughts can form a long cycle of thinking that can feel hard to break away from. Thinking ahead to potential "what if" situations or scenarios can cause the feelings of anxiety to dance uncomfortably through your body, leaving you feeling a sense of panic, fear, worry or being on edge. Do you find yourself thinking thoughts about "what if" that relate to possible future-based situations?

The problem with "what if" thinking is that you can think of situation after situation that keeps looping around from one thought to the next, which just feeds the feelings of anxiety in your body, making them stronger. Getting lost in your thoughts and going ahead into the future or back to the past can overpoweringly disturb the ease and freedom of the present moment. You may feel unable to detach from your repetitive "what if" thoughts. Your personal circumstances may feel unavoidable to detach from; however, mental ease and a reduction in your anxious feelings can be experienced by shifting your focus from within, to anything outside of your mind. "Taking your mind off" the things that you are thinking can give an immediate release to the feelings in your body; this comes through your awareness of where you are with your thoughts, firstly identifying that you are in the pattern or loop of repetitive thinking and therefore anxious feelings, before consciously shifting to being more mentally present.

In the present moment you can feel free, mentally and emotionally. It is in the present moment where there is a sense of ease, freedom, relief and also control that you can experience by directing the focus of your mind.

The method I'm going to share with you encourages you to use your senses to become more mentally present with your focus and your thoughts. This can help you to move away from any limiting, distracting, anxious or "what if" thoughts that consume your focus and cause you to feel anxiety.

This is one of the most common techniques that I use with my clients and students, and I encourage them to make use of it in their day-to-day life. This is a process that allows you to interrupt the thought patterns and cycle of thinking that is pulling you deeper and further into your mind and your thoughts, which is increasing the feelings and experience of anxiety within your body. As most anxious people tend to overthink and spend a lot of time in their mind with their thoughts and in their body with a cyclone of uncomfortable feelings, this method can very rapidly change and transform how you feel for the better. The key is to firstly be aware of your thought processes, to then choose to activate being mindful and present, and to then embrace and prolong the process so that you can actively notice the difference in how you are feeling. The more that you practise this method, the easier it will become for you to change how you are feeling for the better. There are endless opportunities each day, in various spaces and during any time where you can step out of your anxious thoughts and into the ease of being sensory aware and more mentally present.

I most recently taught this method to one of my clients from the TV show *Made in Chelsea* and their response, having taken them through the process, was, "How have you made me feel so calm and present so quickly?" It's actually quite simple. Let's break it down as this is a key part of the Anxiety Antidote.

EXERCISE: HOW TO FEEL
PRESENT IN 60 SECONDS

First read over the method and then practise it a minimum of five times.

METHOD:

1. Begin by looking at one single object in the room that you are in. Focus firstly on what you can see. Look at the colours, the shapes, the textures. See as much as you can and focus on that external object with your eyes. Try this now for around 20 seconds.

2. Now listen to the sounds around you as you continue to view the object. Hear the sounds in your environment and even beyond your environment. See and hear now for 20 seconds.

3. As you continue to see and hear, now sense the feeling of the temperature on your skin. Without touching or looking, feel the fabric of your clothing against your skin. Feel the seat beneath you and the floor underneath your feet. Feel and sense now for 20 seconds.

4. Take your eyes to a different object and repeat the process. See, hear and feel.

5. You can now try this looking out of a window or standing outside in your garden/outside space if it is available. See, hear and feel.

Make sure to practise a minimum of five times.

This technique allows you to be where you are mentally, not just physically. Quite often your body can be physically in one space, but mentally you can be distant and ahead in the future. The key is to use your surroundings to practise being mindfully aware and present with your body. The more that you fine-tune your senses to **see**, **hear** and **feel**, wherever you are, and wherever you are choosing to focus, the easier it will become for you to distance yourself from the activity of overthinking. The process is allowing you to shift your conscious focus with your thoughts to simply, but very effectively, join your body in the present space that you are in.

Your body is not in the future, and it hasn't gone back to the past; it is only your thoughts that can wander off in these directions for long periods of time. As you shift your mind and your thinking to being more present, you may quickly find as you focus on the space that you're in that you can feel, appreciate and embrace the freedom of the present moment that your body always resides in. Consider this as locating your personal GPS. If you had a flashing blue dot on a map which identified where you were physically located, would your mind be in that space with your physical body, or would it have drifted away into the future or past to think various thoughts that are then feeding anxious feelings into your present body? As you see, hear and feel the space around you by using your eyes, ears and ability to feel, you can bring your mind back to your physical location. Notice how you feel as you shift from your thoughts to being more aligned in the present moment.

These personal GPS reminders will appear throughout the book, reminding you to check in with yourself.

You can apply this method more widely, using it at any time and in any environment.

Ask yourself:

- What can I notice and **see** around me?
- What sounds can I **hear** outside of me, that are not my anxious thoughts?
- What can I **feel** without actually reaching to touch with my hands?

These questions will help you change the direction of your thoughts and help you focus on the task of seeing, hearing and feeling the present moment. You can only focus on one thing or one area at a time; it's not possible to think about your anxious thoughts and about what you are going to cook for dinner at the same time. So, these questions can help you utilize your senses to bring you to a more present space.

Try the method now, where you are, and practise it five times, perhaps moving around to experience different environments. This repetition will help you to feel the shift and understand the benefits of this exercise. Experience what it feels like to **see**, **hear** and **feel**, being mentally with your body in the place that you stand, walk or sit.

It is highly likely that you heard sounds that are around you that you may not have been focused on. You may have noticed the depths of colours or detail in what you looked at. You may have felt more stillness in your body as you sensed your feet and the temperature on your skin, all of which can change the direction of your focus very quickly.

Feel the shift from being inside a world of thinking and feeling to where the outside world welcomes you into a place of stillness and freedom. Perhaps outside in nature you can appreciate the subtle beauty and stillness that is around you, which is what you are creating and experiencing within yourself, leading you to very quickly feel more mindful of where you are.

Anxiety on the inside with your thoughts and feelings cannot be experienced in the place of stillness that can be observed and lived in as you **see**, **hear** and **feel**. The opportunity to practise this method daily is yours to choose. You can **see**, **hear** and **feel** any environment. When you are socially with friends, use your senses and be where you are. When you are commuting, walk in the world around you and not the world of your thoughts. When you become aware that you are feeling anxious, reduce the thinking and feeling to become more aware of all that you can **see**, **hear** and **feel** in the space and freedom of your present place.

REALIGN

Time spent overthinking is time spent over-feeling. As you practise being present by bringing your mind into the present space and place where your body is, see it, hear it, feel it, and you can quickly become one with it.

LOOK AT THE
BIG PICTURE

What would you do in the following situations?

1. Your phone battery is on 1% and about to die. Do you:
    a) Immediately plug it in to charge?
    b) Spend time thinking about charging it?
    c) Carry on using it and not care?
    d) Take no action at all?

2. You accidently cut yourself with a knife while cooking. Do you:
    a) Immediately apply a plaster?
    b) Watch yourself bleed and think about helping yourself?
    c) Carry on cooking while bleeding?
    d) Take no action at all and continue to bleed?

3. You find you have a flat tyre on your car or bike. Do you:
    a) Stop and get it fixed immediately?
    b) Spend time thinking about getting it repaired or replaced?
    c) Hope for the best?
    d) Take no action and continue to drive or ride with a flat tyre for as long as possible?

4. You are experiencing anxiety. Do you:

a) Try to deal with it immediately, either personally or with professional help?
b) Try to ignore it even though you're aware of what you're feeling?
c) Pretend it's not there?
d) Live with the uncomfortable feelings for as long as possible and avoid addressing the issue?

As you may have realized from your answers to these questions, there are some problems in life that you will generally tend to take immediate and urgent action to fix or improve, and the same should be said for how you respond to issues with your mental and emotional health.

The truth is that you will only ever get the results that you want in your life by actively working on bringing those specific outcomes into your reality. Without action, practice, commitment and most importantly patience, the life you want will remain an idea only. It is very common for people to heal, address and fix things with great urgency in their day-to-day lives but to not act on working on their mind and emotions. Bottling up their thoughts and feelings can feel overly difficult to experience within, but this doesn't have to be the case.

How long have you been experiencing your anxiety? I've heard from and worked with people who have had anxiety for months, others years, and a few people have told me that they have put up with feeling anxious for over 20 years. The next part of the antidote is to create a personal assessment of how exactly you have been experiencing your anxiety. Let's begin with a few questions that will allow you to reflect on this. Consider writing your answers down if that helps you to express your thoughts better.

1. When did you first start feeling anxious?
2. What is your anxiety in relation to specifically?
3. Was there a specific event/experience in your life that caused you to feel anxious?
4. How often do you experience your anxiety?
5. How long does a period of anxiety last?
6. When do you not experience anxiety?
7. What are you doing when you are not experiencing anxiety?
8. What professional help (if any) have you had to overcome your anxiety?
9. What action are you personally taking (if any), in addition to reading this book, to help you improve your anxiety?

Sometimes taking a step back to look at a situation can help you realize that enough is enough, and that there's no more time or life experiences to be missed at the hands of your anxious thoughts, feelings and emotions. Were you aware of the amount of time and the ways that anxiety has ruled your life, or was this new learning to you?

Whether or not you've already taken steps to make improvements regarding your mind and emotions, it's always important to get a clear understanding of the outcome you want in your life. This is like getting precise on the destination that you want to reach on a journey. With a clear idea of your destination in mind, you will feel more motivated to take action to move from where you currently are, so you can get to where you actually want to be in your life. It can act as a driving force that helps you to keep pushing towards that desired destination, reminding you through any difficult times of anxiety to not give up on working on yourself. From an NLP point of view, a clear well-formed outcome can help drive you to an experience that you feel aligned with, which you feel compelled to then manifest.

So, consider the following questions:

1. What specifically do you want to achieve with your anxiety?
2. When do you want to have your specific outcome?
3. Consider what your outcome looks like and sounds like. Can you imagine yourself living the way you want to live, anxiety-free?
4. Take some time to explore your outcome in your mind.
5. How will your life improve when your anxiety is gone or more under control?
6. What will your life look like when you achieve your outcome?
7. What kind of things will you say to yourself with your inner voice when you have your outcome?
8. What do you need to do to get your desired outcome?
9. How much action do you need to take and how often?

10. Are you willing to put the time, effort, and commitment into achieving your outcome?

Your anxiety may at times have left you unable to think beyond the present thoughts, feelings and emotions that captivate you. Having a clear picture of your desired destination is always going to help motivate your mind and body into acting on healing the feelings within, especially in any times of overwhelming anxiety. You can use your desired outcome as a reminder of what you are working towards. It's important to actively use your mind to focus on the outcome that you want as your reality. This is partly achieved through visualization but also by using your inner voice to hear your thoughts as well as see them. As you see the images in your mind, visualizing how you want your life to be beyond your anxiety, and as you hear your thoughts directing you to that desired mental destination, you should feel a shift in your body for how you're feeling. In building on this internal experience, you can get greater clarity on the outcome that you want which can help you to expand your thinking and help keep you motivated to keep working on and through your anxiety experience. The clearer your outcome is in your mind, the more focused you may find yourself. Once you have that clarity, you then must action the steps required to move yourself forward to your desired reality, but remember it always starts with your thoughts.

EXPLAINING THE UNKNOWN

Have you ever tried to explain to someone how you're feeling when you're anxious, or perhaps tried to tell them what you're experiencing inside of yourself, but failed to find the right words? Explaining how you feel to someone when you don't even understand it yourself can leave you feeling frustrated and even more uncomfortable within yourself, which can just add to your anxiety. From my work, another major concern for my clients is the inability to be able to control what their own body is doing. As your body is your permanent physical home, it can feel overwhelmingly uncomfortable when your body experiences any physical symptoms. Feeling comfortable in your own skin, at ease in your own body is something that can be experienced as a normal and natural state, a state that you don't have to think so much about. In the uncertainty of knowing when you may feel anxious or how strong an anxiety episode may be, it can be exhausting thinking through every "what if" situation in relation to any of the physical symptoms in any possible strength that may take over your body in any time and any place.

My intention of this next section is for you to be able to identify and understand for **yourself** a deeper understanding of your anxiety. This will help you to get more specific on what you need to work on in your life and help eliminate confusion. It will also help you increase and improve your communication to relieve the pressure you may have felt in finding the right words to explain what you are experiencing. Knowing where to start, what to say and how to say it can feel as exhausting as feeling your anxious feelings.

THE PHYSICAL EXPERIENCE

Each and every individual will have common patterns that are similar to the next person's anxiety experience, but also parts that are individual and unique. I'm going to share with you some of the physical symptoms I have had myself, and some common patterns that have been communicated to me from the people that I have worked with, which might help you to reflect on your own experience of anxiety.

BODY SWEATS

Whether it's sweaty palms, armpits, foreheads or various areas of your body, you may have experienced your body uncontrollably sweating when you're feeling anxious. Each person can have a different physical experience in relation to body sweats, and some people do not experience this when they're anxious. You may have even noticed sweaty palms or a rise in your body temperature before you even realize you're anxious. I have experienced only sweaty palms when I am anxious, but in others I have witnessed sweat running down their forehead, and visible sweat patches upon their clothing. It can feel uncomfortable, embarrassing and uncontrollable.

Why do you sweat when you're anxious? Anxiety can cause the body to secrete the "fight or flight" hormones that prepare you to take action – a physical response to your thoughts going one hundred miles an hour in your mind! As a result of a rising body temperature, your body tries to keep you cool by sweating. It can be a stressful, embarrassing and an uncomfortable experience.

SHALLOW BREATHING

I've described it as "panic" breathing as it is a rhythm that is usually short, sharp and quick, as opposed to a more normal breathing rate, or a slower rate that is experienced during relaxation. If you were to be in the "panic" breathing mode all day long, you would simply hyperventilate. It's not comfortable or possible to live through each day on short, sharp, quick breaths. In your normal state, your breathing will be naturally slower, possibly deeper and generally more relaxed. You probably won't even notice the speed, flow or rhythm of your breath when you are going about your day-to-day life; however, you're probably more aware of it and hear it loud and clear when you're experiencing anxiety. Anxious breathing tends to be higher up in the chest as opposed to more relaxed breathing which can be located lower down towards your navel. It can be quicker and shorter, which can leave you feeling as though you can't breathe. The shortness of breath will be contributing to your anxiety as you physically feel the restrictions of your high chest, short breathing pattern that can leave you feeling like you're panicking to breathe. For some individuals this alone can be overwhelming, where the anxiety can potentially lead to a physical panic attack.

INCREASED HEARTRATE

Nothing can make you feel on the edge of your seat quicker than a fast heart rate. "*It feels like my heart is going to come out of my chest,*" I've heard people say. As you hear each beat sounding like a thunderous thud that appears to get louder with each breath, your sense of sound can become hypnotized by your fast beating heart. The sound can propel you deep into fear as the central point of your existence may sound and feel as though its unable to cope in your body. The increased heart rate is a response to threat, whether in the physical situation you are experiencing or in your thoughts. Again, it is your mind and body entering into a potential "fight or flight" mode, affecting the autonomic nervous system, which leaves you with the physical experience of feeling out of control of your own body.

MUSCULAR REACTIONS

Feeling tight, tense and rigid in one's body is another physical symptom that is experienced by many who suffer from anxiety. You may find that you grip your hands tightly, your shoulders become raised and tense, the facial muscles and jaw can tighten, or your whole body may feel rigid and stuck. The body can freeze and you may feel unable to move at all. These symptoms may go unnoticed if your focus is dominated by your overactive thoughts, your increased heart rate and shallow breathing. However, you may at times be overly aware of the trembling that can happen in your body. With your legs feeling like jelly, the overwhelming physical experience of anxiety can literally wipe you off your feet.

GUT CHURNING

The rollercoaster ride of anxiety can turn your gut more than a tumble drier. It's quite fascinating how you can look and appear as if all is well and good on the outside, while on the inside you can feel overwhelmingly turbulent. You may have experienced your stomach "in knots", and at times it may feel like it's "churning". You may even feel nauseous. For some individuals, the experience of anxiety in their gut can leave them feeling socially anxious and impact how they interact with others and how often they leave the house. Once again, this symptom of anxiety is influenced by the impact of anxiety on the autonomic nervous system.

BOWEL MOVEMENTS

The waves of anxiety throughout the body can very much impact the control or lack of control on one's bowel movements. You may at times have experienced this yourself. From flatulence, accidents in your underwear, to *Mission Impossible*-style sprints to the bathroom, the effect of anxiety on your bowel movements can be more than potentially embarrassing.

I was recently sat with a friend at a birthday lunch who unfortunately, in the space of an afternoon meal, had to leave the table three times to go to the bathroom because of their anxiety, and a lot of the people that I have worked with have been motivated to seek help due to the fear of not having a bathroom available should they experience an anxious episode. This fear has negatively stopped them leaving the house, left them with worry when travelling and altered their lives in ways that are a far cry from the simplicity that they once knew. One thing that you will always want to feel certain of is that you can comfortably find a restroom with control, comfort and ease. The need for this certainty can leave you feeling on edge in a high state of anxiety.

UNDERSTANDING THE POSSIBLE ROOT CAUSES OF YOUR ANXIETY

A SIGN OF UNDERLYING ISSUES?

The uncertainty over something you have no control over can leave you feeling mentally and physically on the edge of your seat. When anxious, it can for a long time feel as though you're trying in vain to catch yourself from falling. This uncertainty can feel exhausting. Parts of your life that you are experiencing, whether it be your relationship, your job, a situation socially or even the health of someone that you love, can leave you feeling anxious as your mind becomes consumed with the unknown. You can end up mentally distracted from the present moment and emotionally drained from the weight of your mind. As your uncertainty lies outside of your control, the distraction from the anxiety that you feel can unpleasantly rob you from the freedom and ease of the present moment.

Then there's the feeling of uncertainty where you are anxious for no apparent reason. Yes, that makes sense, and for some of you, you will know this experience all too well. This is the anxiety that you feel where it comes out of nowhere and takes over your body, emotionally leaving you feeling uneasy in your own skin, without you knowing why. There can be instances where you are fine, loving life, feeling good and then out of nowhere, and for reasons that you can't think of, you may feel and then experience anxiety, and not know how to stop the uncomfortable feelings within. If this sounds like you, the root of this type of anxiety could be unconscious. Your unconscious mind stores and records all of the experiences that you have had in your life, and anxiety can be imprinted from past experiences that you may have forgotten or even been too young to remember. Because your mind's role is to protect you and to preserve your health, it may be repressing the experience. If this type of anxiety is surfacing for you, it is likely a sign that there are underlying repressed emotions that are calling for your attention with the desire to be released.

A LEARNED BEHAVIOUR?

"*I've always been a worrier.*" This is a common declaration I hear from a lot of people that I work with. It's usually followed by, "*I've been this way for as long as I can remember.*" I then go on to ask: "When you were growing up, was there anybody in your household that experienced anxiety?" The answer is usually "*yes*". Now this isn't a time to point the finger and assign blame to a parent, guardian or sibling for the anxiety that you may be presently experiencing, but from my professional experience, some individuals have communicated that they did grow up with an individual in their household who "was always anxious". In our early years, around the age of seven years old onwards we learn and develop through what is known in the NLP world as "modelling". Now you may have dressed up like your favourite pop star or superhero, but were there times in those early years where you began to express your worry like mum or dad or generally any of their demonstrated behaviour? You may not have realized it but for a lot of people it is common to "model" the behaviour of those around them. During these formative years, your beliefs may have through experience been positively shaped by what you were told, what you were taught and from what you experienced, which could have led you to unconsciously run some of these patterns currently in your adult life. It is common as a practitioner to hear clients talk about how their parent used to worry, or tell them to always be safe, or prevent them from taking part in things because of their fears, which are now beliefs and actions that, upon reflection in their sessions, they can now identify as something they now themselves do as adults. This is a very normal and natural pattern that can be experienced as adults. The people that taught you, brought you up and spent time with you as a youngster will have influenced the way in which you experience the world today. In identifying if your anxiety could possibly be a learned behaviour, you may find relief in knowing that change is possible, as is learning new behaviours that leave you feeling more in control and at ease.

AN EXPERT IN CATASTROPHISING

"*You name it, I've thought it. Every worse-case scenario I have thought up.*" This is another example of how clients have expressed their anxiety experience. One of the main challenges with this experience is that the individual is often unaware of the emotional impact the mind has on the body. In thinking through every possible threat, every potential disaster, the individual has then switched on the negative and uncomfortable feelings of anxiety within their body. These feelings are created from what you are thinking. From what you see inside your mind with your mental movies and thoughts formed with pictures, to what you say and communicate to yourself with your inner voice. As you think yourself ahead in time to the possible scenes and scenarios that live out inside your mind, you simply yet powerfully remove yourself from the present moment as you experience the emotional pain that your mind wonders off to experience. This pattern of thinking can go on for long periods of time. You may even frequently find yourself distracted from the present and thinking only of the worst possible outcomes. This is never helpful, as thinking the worst is going to leave you feeling at your worst, and in the end you are in some ways contributing to your own suffering, through your thinking. The more time and energy you spend thinking these thoughts, which leave your body feeling the impact of your mind, the more normal and natural this pattern of thinking can then become for you. Over a long period of time, this can end up as your normal state, where thinking these types of thoughts and feeling these types of anxiety induced feelings, can be felt as the only way you know how to be. The key to transforming how you feel and moving past your anxiety, is to work on your mind and with your thoughts on a daily basis to change and transform your mental and emotional reality for the better.

Importantly, do not feel alone in your experience, as the way that you may have felt uneasy in your body has likely been felt by another individual – or even hundreds if not thousands of others.

REAL TALK

What lives in the mind is felt in the body. What you see in your thoughts, you will feel. What you say to yourself, dictates your inner environment. Your mind is the director of your life and your thoughts, for what you see and say will always set the ever-changing tones of your inner space, world and universe. Understand the connection, seek the patterns – and rewrite the script.

CHANGE
POSITIONS

There can be a number of positions that you find yourself in when you're feeling anxious. Considering the following positions, think about where you may be when you're often experiencing your anxiety and whether there is a better position to move yourself to that will help you improve your anxiety for the better.

Position 1: I am aware that I am experiencing anxiety and I have no idea how to deal with the anxiety that I am experiencing. *Are you here?*

Position 2: I am aware that I am experiencing anxiety and I have a few ways that I know that can help me to improve how I am feeling, but I am not taking any practical action for myself or making use of the tools that I know about. *Is this true for you?*

Position 3: I am aware that I am experiencing anxiety and I am putting to use techniques that I know of that do help me to improve how I feel within, and I am also trying new ways and methods that I have yet to experience. I am also feeling a positive shift and change from the work I am putting in myself. *What does this allow you to feel?*

Position 4: I am aware that I am experiencing anxiety and I am putting to use techniques that I know of. However, I am not experiencing any relief and my anxiety is still there. *Are you ready to experience more possibilities?*

It is important to reiterate that these positions are not fixed. You will have good days and challenging days. One of the key factors in you overpowering your anxiety is to understand that you can actively change your position with regards to your anxiety by utilizing any of the skills outlined throughout this book to help you change and improve your position when anxious. Let's explore in more detail each position to help you better understand where your power lies.

POSITION 1

The common pattern that I see in position I is where individuals will feel as though they are suffering at the hands of their anxiety, and feel unable to change and improve things for the better. In this position they may be unaware of any way to cope with their thoughts and emotions, and it can often feel as though the anxiety is happening to them: they often feel they have no control over how they are thinking or feeling. They tend to be aware of how anxious they feel, how unpleasant the feelings can be and mentally they will be deep within their own thoughts. There may be a lot of personal inner dialogue to themselves about the situation that they feel anxious about. They may also spend a lot of time thinking ahead to the future, mentally seeing pictures and mental movies inside their thoughts of the situations that they watch over, which causes them to feel anxious. It is in position one where the individual may be new to the anxiety they are experiencing. It may be their first time that they are experiencing the physical symptoms of anxiety, physically feeling very uncomfortable.

They may feel unsure of what is happening to them and may not themselves be aware that they are anxious but confused to why they feel the way that they feel.

On the other hand, individuals in this position may know these anxious feelings extremely well. They may have experienced them for weeks, months, if not years, on and off or even daily. They may have become overly familiar with the experience of anxiety and see it as their normal and natural daily state.

Both positions can feel overwhelming if the anxiety is left untreated. Aware or unaware, the situation will only improve if the person takes action, alone or with professional help, to work on their anxiety. For the person who has not taken any action and that has lived with the anxiety for a short or even a prolonged period of time, the anxiety may have affected their life, from their health, relationships, social interactions and even professional life as they have tried to mask or juggle the feelings they experience within. The longer the anxiety is left, the stronger it can become, and the individual can experience a sense of exhaustion as well as a variety of negative feelings from repressing the anxiety inside of themselves. It is in this position where people will either take immediate action and work on themselves or with a professional to help them feel better, or they will struggle on the inside with the anxiety experience, where the struggle lasts as long as the person chooses to experience the inner conflict. This can be weeks, months, years and, from professional experience, even decades. I have encountered various individuals who have found great relief for their anxiety within a single 90-minute coaching session using

NLP, who have then questioned why they have not sought help for so long.

If you are in this first position, consider: *How long have you been feeling and experiencing your anxiety? How long have you not dealt with the feelings? How has the anxiety affected any area of your life?*

Then consider: *How do you want to feel? How do you want to live? What action do you need to take to deal with your anxiety? What would your future self, 10 years wiser and older, advise you to do in relation to your anxiety?*

POSITION 2

In position 2, individuals are aware that they are at times experiencing anxiety. They are also aware of some methods that they can utilize themselves to improve the way that they are feeling within, however they are not taking any action. I work with various individuals who often communicate that they have seen another or several professionals, they have read self-help books, some have even spent thousands travelling across the world having been on retreat-style programmes, but **they do not put the time or work into improving how they feel**. This resistance can be down to a number of things. One area I often consider is that the individual may not be communicating or addressing the root issue that is causing them to feel anxious. They may be out of alignment with their core values, and even unaware of their core values, which then leads them to feel anxious. This type of anxiety comes under unconscious anxiety. Exploring a wider picture of their life can help potentially uncover areas that they may have been unaware of that are then causing them to feel anxious.

Another factor here could be that change requires effort. To transform your body, lose weight or increase your flexibility all takes time and effort. Improving your diet also needs planning and dedicated action. For a lot of people, the expectation of a quick fix can demotivate them in putting the work into their own personal healing, which can leave the person's anxiety to grow inside of themselves in destructive strength.

If you are in this second position, consider: *How long have you been feeling and experiencing your anxiety? How long have you not dealt with the feelings? How has the anxiety affected any area of your life?*

Then consider: *How do you want to feel? How do you want to live? What action do you need to take to deal with your anxiety? What would your future self, 10 years wiser and older, advise you to do in relation to your anxiety?*

POSITION 3

Position 3 is where the magic happens. It is here where individuals will be aware that they are experiencing anxiety and are using the tools they are equipped with to work on dealing with their symptoms. They may be working with a professional, using guided audios to help them breathe, direct their focus and be more present, or even practising self-care with activities like mindfulness, journaling or exercise. In this position, the person may be aware of the elements of their life that trigger their anxiety. They may have situations personally, professionally, on-going relationship and even social challenges that they use their skills to help them relieve the symptoms that they feel. This is also the position where the individual may continue to learn about their mental and emotional health in whatever way works best for them, as they take their power into their own hands to help improve the overall aspects of their life.

If you are in this third position, consider: *How has working on your anxiety improved your life for the better? How much time is required for you to feel at ease and in control when you're anxious? How has your life benefited from you personally developing these skills to help your anxiety?*

Then consider: *How will your life continue to improve if you stay focused and on track? What would your future self, 10 years wiser and older, advise you to do in relation to your anxiety?*

POSITION 4

Position 4 is an area where some individuals will not feel any change or any major relief from their anxiety. They may be actively working on their anxiety utilizing a variety of methods on a daily basis. They may be working alongside a programme or with a practitioner and they may still not feel or experience any relief that they feel is enough to help shift them from their experience of anxiety. In this position they may not consciously be aware of why they are anxious and what is causing their anxiety. For this individual, further exploration on an unconscious level with a suitable practitioner would likely be useful. Regression work to a younger age may be used to help the individual explore the possibilities of their past that may be causing them to feel anxious. It could be highly likely that this individual has experienced mild to severe trauma in the past. They may have had frequent panic attacks or experiences in the past that were huge ordeals, yet they detached from their feelings and emotions. The unconscious memories and experiences may be repressed from conscious awareness, yet the feelings may be consciously present, leaving the person overwhelmed and confused. An experienced practitioner, in particular offering Integral Eye Movement Therapy (IEMT, see Further Resources, page 216), a process that I often use with clients, may be able to help you join the dots, heal and overcome the difficulties of the past.

These positions are not fixed. You can end up switching positions and moving from being proactive to procrastinating to even allowing your anxiety to take over. This could be down to the confusion that you think and feel in trying to understand and even cope with what's happening inside of you. In trying to understand your anxiety it may help you feel more proactive in taking your anxiety on to make things feel better for how you then live your life. Understanding that you may move positions with how you deal with anxiety, that you may have some good days and some challenging days is all part of the journey of healing your anxiety, and it is hugely important to notice any changes that you experience for the better when working on your anxiety. As you continue now to identify the possible common patterns of your anxiety, the positions you may move between when dealing with your anxiety, you may find some further clarity on the specific definitions of some of the patterns of anxiety you may be experiencing.

NEW POSITIONS

If you look out of the window, you see a world that exists outside of your mind and body. As you move your body, you engage your mind. In becoming unstuck, you can actively move the many positions of your thinking that lead you to new doorways, new pathways, new experiences that shift you from this to whatever may possibly be, which is freeing beyond the freeze of anxiety.

PATTERNS
OF ANXIETY

To help you to gain a deeper understanding of your anxiety, I'm going to provide a brief summary of a variety of anxiety disorders. It is my personal opinion that we can think of the following examples as anxiety **states** that do have the potential to be overcome with the right effective help. The sections that follow include suggestions for "how to heal". You can follow my guidance for writing lists, using your inner voice, and changing your thought patterns from what is suggested. These suggestions and exercises are introductions to ideas and ways to work on these specific anxiety areas, and you will make more sense of the suggestions from the methods that are covered later in the book in the **"self-action"** section, but you can now give consideration to what is suggested.

GENERALIZED ANXIETY DISORDER (GAD)

Generalized anxiety disorder is where you may experience feelings of anxiety, uncertainty and even worry for various areas of your life. This may include feelings of panic, fear, worry and elements of overthinking. Your anxiety may be for other people, family, friends and loved ones, it may be for yourself in relation to the things that you do where you feel anxious or worry over day-to-day situations and experiences you may possibly encounter. Generalized anxiety may be something that's new to you or may be a feeling that you have experienced for a long period of time. In this state of anxiety, you may vary from feeling low-level anxiety that appears to have always being there as a feeling that lingers around, or something that can grow in strength when certain things cause you to feel overly anxious. Your general day-to-day experience may be one where you focus on what you worry or fear, where you think through areas of your life that cause you to feel concerned and it may have been weeks or even months where you've felt a sense of relaxation.

GAD MINDSET

You may find yourself thinking through various "what if" situations and scenarios for the day, week or even further ahead. You may at times find yourself watching mental movies through your thoughts where you consider the worse-case scenarios and situations that could possibly happen later in time. You may even have inner dialogue where you communicate with yourself or even listen to a voice inside your own head that is expressing anxiety, thinking through future-based thoughts. In most situations you may think through a variety of options for what you are doing, preplanning areas of safety or possible threats. You may find relief momentarily whilst thinking about one situation and then feeling less anxious about that particular situation, however your thoughts may then move to another area to fixate on where this pattern of thinking continues, prolonging the feelings of anxiety. You may at times be in good company, feel relaxed, be in the moment with who you are with and with what you are doing, and then out of nowhere you may begin to hear the voice of anxiety, or become distracted in watching over the thoughts that play out in your head of worse-case scenarios that immediately rob you of the present moment.

CASE STUDY

"I constantly worry about everything," a client said to me in his first coaching session. This had been his pattern for the last five years, where he had found himself continually considering the worst-possible outcomes for various areas of his life. Whether it was his children and their futures, his job, the prospects of his finances to general life spending, he couldn't remember the last time he felt relaxed. He even communicated how he worried about the money he was spending for his sessions that were to help with his anxiety, as he considered where else he may need to use that money and also the possible negative impacts on his family if they were to run out of money. From school fees, holidays to maintaining his home, money was a big source of his daily anxiety.

His fixation on money had started once he became a father, when he found himself constantly worrying about how to support his family. Even though he was in a stable and successful job, he was suddenly negatively overthinking about the future, focusing only on potential problems. This not only left him feeling anxious, but the fixation soon spread to considering the worst on a daily basis – and not only in relation to his finances. He would think through possible accidents for activities his children were taking part in; possible health conditions he may develop, which could lead him to die; possible natural disasters or terrorist attacks in crowded places that he or his family may attend – all of which filled him with anxiety.

His anxious thoughts affected him not only physically, but in ways that impacted his day-to-day life. He struggled to be present with the company he kept, he felt exhausted by the constant worrying, and he even struggled to sleep.

HOW TO HEAL

Consider what specifically you are getting anxious about. Write a list of the areas of your life that are causing you to feel anxious. The list may include health, family, finances, employment, etc. Now, for each area, mark out of 10 how strong the anxiety is, 10 being the highest.

Now think of times **when you don't feel anxious**. What are you doing when you are not anxious? Write a list of the times you're not anxious and what you are doing in those times, so you counterbalance your focus of only noticing the times you're anxious. How are you thinking when you are not anxious? What do you see in your mind and what do you hear with your inner voice when you're not anxious?

The key here with GAD is to use your awareness to override the thought patterns and inner dialogue that is causing you to feel anxious. Options for breaking the cycle of generalized anxious thoughts will follow, but making your lists and observing your thoughts is a good place to start. You can write daily lists and read over the lists to highlight to your mind any examples of times you are not anxious. This can help expand your thinking to frequently realise that you have various times daily where you are not anxious.

As you interrupt and disturb the anxiety patterns of thinking, then practise being mindful to feel fully present and relaxed with your **Personal GPS**: see, hear and feel the present moment to shift from your anxious thoughts.

Consider then developing more empowering and reassuring thought processes to install a new way of thinking and living for the better. Install a more reassuring and affirming inner voice where you list five to ten statements that you could speak back through your thoughts to break the anxious pattern and to feel more assured within. If you feel or are aware that your GAD is triggered by past difficult memories, or overwhelming feelings of guilt, regret, shame, anger, frustration, sadness or low self-esteem, it could be one or two of these listed; consider some one-to-one professional help through the process of Integral Eye Movement Therapy for a more personal and rapid transformation.

HEALTH ANXIETY

One of the most common areas of anxiety I have worked with professionally is with people who have an ongoing health issue. Whether they are ill or having treatment for a condition, they can experience anxiety relating to their health. Other individuals may also experience anxiety for their health even if they are not actually ill. Anxiety for possible future-based illnesses is something that a lot of people will experience as they worry for their future that they may one day get sick. For the people who have a diagnosed condition that they are living with or are having treatment for, their anxiety can be a daily struggle. Each person is different in what they feel anxious for in relation to their health. It could be their physical health, worry regarding treatment and medication, fear for the worst-possible outcomes for loved ones and family, whom they feel they can't fully care for or support. Whatever the cause of the concern, anxiety can add to the physical discomfort you are experiencing which can add to the challenge of feeling better mentally and emotionally. One of the difficulties in overcoming health anxiety is that the body can change daily with regards to the symptoms that are being experienced in the mind and body. Added to this, doctors' visits, test results, lack of improvement and even a worsening in one's condition can leave you in a heightened state of anxiety.

HEALTH ANXIETY MINDSET

You may feel completely dissociated from the present moment where you struggle to be anywhere but in the world of your thoughts. Even though you are working on your body and health through attempting to heal your body, you may mentally feel as though you are out of your body feeling detached, and overly in the space of your thoughts. At times you may wander off into the future, thinking a variety of outcomes that leave you feeling emotionally low, fearful and even angry. Your emotions may move quickly through the day. The more you overthink, the more emotions you will find yourself feeling. At times you may be so occupied with your thoughts that you find yourself distant from your body as you step out of the physical symptoms of unease, yet you find yourself deep in the discomfort of your mind. Overthinking the future, the worse-case possible scenarios and not being present is something that may leave you feeling detached from life. It may feel like an effort to think positively, to turn your focus to hope and healing; however, it can feel like a relief within your body as you direct your awareness away from your anxious thoughts.

CASE STUDY

A young healthy mother of three came to see me at my clinic for an anxiety coaching session with regards to her health. This lady was actually in good health however, her anxiety was around constantly fretting that she would get sick and not be able to look after her children. She even feared the worst: that she may die and not see her children grow up. Even though she was healthy with no symptoms of any illness, and no diagnosis of any illness from a medical professional, she would often find herself checking her body for possible signs of cancer. This would lead her to have anxiety attacks where she felt overwhelmed from the threat of possibly getting ill where she would even visit doctors and have blood tests done to check that she didn't have cancer. As her mind and emotions raced from thinking she had cancer, to checking her body, from the wait for doctors' appointments, to times where she waited for results, anxiety for her health was something that she had experienced for years. This pattern of behaviour became obsessive for this lady and had grown stronger over time.

One gentleman I worked with became increasingly anxious after having suffered a back injury. A slipped disc led him to need time off work, where he fell behind with deadlines. After working with an osteopath and Pilates instructor, he became stronger, more aligned and had increased flexibility; however, he experienced daily anxiety that he would once again injure his back. This anxiety transformed the way he lived. He would not carry a thing, which annoyed his wife – particularly when travelling – and he also lost interest in sex. He also became overly cautious with how he moved and how he interacted with his children, lessening his affection towards them from fear he may twist or bend in a way that might lead to a back injury.

HOW TO HEAL

Self-talk is something that we all naturally engage in, so learn to develop a positive inner voice. From the moment you open your eyes in the morning, begin by activating your inner voice in a positive manner with at least 10 sentences or phrases where you thank your body for all of the positive functions that it performs for you daily. You may even want to picture and imagine yourself in perfect health. Having this internal representation of your body in the optimum condition can help redirect your mind to a more positive outcome for you to work towards, shifting your focus away from any thoughts of anxiety.

Consider also practising mindfulness as you activate your **Personal GPS**. This can help you to feel grounded, relaxed and more in the present space with your physical body.

A daily mindfulness practice and working with your inner voice can help you to create more positive feelings and allow you to feel as though you have more control over your mind.

SOCIAL ANXIETY

For some people, social situations can trigger panic, overwhelm and anxiety. Having to meet new people, talk to people that you know in small or large groups, asking for assistance in retail spaces, socializing at work or even at the school gates can lead to various levels of anxiety. One of the most common elements of social anxiety that people experience is a lack of confidence. You may feel unconfident to speak up, fear you won't be heard or that you may be misunderstood or feel anxious from being around a group of people. Avoiding social situations and having time alone may be your preference; however, your social anxiety may over time become stronger the more you shut yourself off from being social, which can become a factor that limits some individuals for the amount of time they have in leaving the house.

SOCIAL ANXIETY MINDSET

With social anxiety, your most common companion will be your inner voice, and the world that you spend most of your time in is on the inside, as the outside can seem like a fearful place. You may find yourself overthinking situations where you may not find the right words to say or may come across in a way that embarrasses you. You might worry about stuttering or stumbling over your words, believing that you will be laughed at or mocked, or being concerned that you may sweat, blush, hyperventilate or look stupid. You may avoid social situations, but often feel regretful or even guilty when you think of the events or socializing that you miss out on.

CASE STUDY

Justin found himself in quite a dilemma, as he wanted to start a relationship but thought he was incredibly shy. He had a small, close circle of friends who he saw less of over the years. He lived behind his computer screen, working for himself and by himself. His time interacting with people decreased as time went on, and he was happy in the world that he lived in.

The trigger for his anxiety came when some of his small circle of friends had started relationships, some even getting engaged. The prospect of now spending time with the boys also meant there would be female company in his small circle. He also wanted a relationship, but the idea of dating filled him with dread. Justin had cancelled dates, which had all started through online communication. He had also stopped seeing his friends as much in person due to the added plus-ones to the small circle he used to feel at home in. As a result, his social anxiety had only become worse.

HOW TO HEAL

Avoid jumping in at the deep end. People who are socially anxious tend to feel more anxiety in larger groups and in busier surroundings. The key is to build up your confidence slowly, so consider starting with smaller numbers for company. Perhaps try one person or possibly two and notice the positive feelings you experience while being out with company. Consider your communication. Talk about your week, your day, what you're watching and ask those you're with questions to keep the conversation flowing. Then in time you can build up to more people in the group. Take yourself out of your comfort zone and meet someone or some people at least once a week to override and work through the anxiety experience.

Also work on your mindset and your thought patterns in relation to feeling anxious. Work with your inner voice to have a more reassuring and confident inner voice that can overpower the voice of anxiety when it comes on. Through your awareness of being in your mind watching the mental movies of your anxious thoughts, switch the channel and watch the best possible outcomes that could happen or thoughts from previous positive social meet-ups that remind you that you do not need to worry as you access feelings of comfort from past positive memories.

PHOBIAS

Phobias are an overwhelming fear of an object, place, situation, feeling or animal. For many individuals the feelings that they experience can be on a spectrum which increases as and when exposed to the potential phobia. The individual can however feel and experience anxiety in relation to the phobia, be it for a future-based possible situation or even a situation that may be something they are taking part in later that day, week or month. A person, for example, may need to take their children to the zoo, but may have a fear of snakes. They can then feel anxious in the lead up to the trip they are going to take, but this, depending on the person, could be a mild anxiety experience. For some it may be more intense anxiety as they may feel anxious that their child may want to visit the reptile section that they as an adult want to avoid. The anxiety for the phobia can escalate in the environment that the person is in. Walking down the street they may feel no anxiety or fear of a snake as the likelihood of encountering a snake is probably very low. Having to walk past enclosed snakes in the zoo can cause the fear of the phobia to intensify or even prevent the individual from stepping foot into the designated area as the anxiety of the future-based possible experience may end up in full strength fear when exposed to the phobia.

PHOBIA MINDSET

The anxiety may be at the back of your mind and very low in its experience or existence when the threat or fear is not around. You may find yourself relaxed and getting on with your life and the anxiety may start to build or appear as you get closer to being exposed to experiencing your phobia. Fear of flying, being around birds, driving on the motorway to being locked in a small space. Your phobia can be non-existent in its feeling of fear when out of sight, however a single thought or sighting in relation to what you may fear can cause the feelings of anxiety to surface very quickly. Thinking the worst through visually thinking through what could possibly happen can leave you sweating and feeling panic. Hearing your inner voice communicate your anxious thoughts as you think about your fear can leave you in an overwhelming state of panic.

CASE STUDY

Monica was a successful lawyer who worked long hours in a job she loved in a huge firm in the city. The building where she worked was spread out over several floors and Monica noticed that she had become fearful of using the lift after she had got stuck in it with a number of colleagues for a few minutes before it naturally moved on. This left her feeling dread whenever she had to enter the small space and therefore she now avoided it at all costs. This was becoming a problem, however, as so much of her work was in different buildings for meetings and she often arrived late and flustered from using the stairs. She also began to notice that she was thinking about avoiding the lift throughout the day and felt anxious about bumping into colleagues in the building who used the lift without any concern at all. The anxious mindset along with the feelings of fear and panic that she experienced in the back of her mind and overwhelmingly in her body, day in, day out, were getting stronger.

HOW TO HEAL

Depending on the level of your phobia, you may require professional assistance. I have seen people's lives change in relation to what they fear within two hours using IEMT, NLP and Hypnosis (see pages 215–16 for more on each of these techniques). Consider how your fear may have affected your life, stopped you from doing certain activities or even impacted those in your immediate family or circle of friends. The internal representations of fear may be formed and constructed as more scary and real that its actual reality. In changing and transforming your relationship with the fear, which can be achieved quickly, you can feel more at ease and able to move forward beyond the limiting thoughts, feelings and experiences that may be holding you back. The methods covered later in the section "Triggered" (page 178) may well help you deal with past difficult experiences and memories that could be the cause of your fear or phobia.

POST-TRAUMATIC STRESS DISORDER (PTSD)

Anxiety can be experienced and developed if you have previously gone through a traumatic ordeal. It may be something that happened recently, which triggers you to be anxious, or it may be a traumatic experience that happened in the past or even in the early years of your life, leading you to now experience anxiety. With past traumatic experiences, some individuals are aware that the experience in some ways causes them to feel and experience anxiety, whereas others have no idea that their anxiety is rooted in the traumatic experience of their past.

PTSD can include flashbacks to parts of the experience, which can be vivid in the way it is pictured in the person's mind. A person may even have nightmares or be presently occupied re-visiting and re-feeling the traumatic experience, where they feel the feelings and impact in their present moment. These flashbacks can come on from out of nowhere and feel hugely overwhelming. Through the traumatic experiences of the past, a person may develop and experience anxiety for future possible difficulties or repeat experiences, as well as anxiety for other areas of their life that may be impacted negatively for how they experience the world because of the impact of their trauma.

PTSD MINDSET

Anxiety may be dominantly what you feel, however at times you may switch from feeling anxious about the day ahead or any other future scenario, to feeling the pain of your past experiences. Feeling present, relaxed, comfortable in your own body can feel like a drop in the ocean. Your thoughts may often be fast as you visit the past, mentally re-watching and physically re-feeling the trauma you encountered. Your mind may also race ahead to the future where you think through possible future-based difficulties that leave you feeling locked in the depths of your difficult emotions. Flashbacks may come from out of nowhere in any time and any place, where your thoughts feel uncontrollable to move beyond.

In other ways, anxiety may be your current reality; however, you may not be consciously aware that the traumatic experiences that were so long ago are triggering you to feel on edge. The past may seem like a distant memory, however your body can hold on to the feelings associated with your trauma, as can your unconscious mind.

CASE STUDY

An individual I worked with who had witnessed an attack on a family member had severe anxiety and underlying PTSD. The person felt anxious about going out of the home, and felt that they could be attacked in a similar way to what had been witnessed. Even normal and relaxing activities, like watching the TV or having dinner at home, left him mentally withdrawn from where he was. He was continually fearing the worst was going to happen to him, picturing it in his mind. He felt on edge even in the most simple and relaxed places as his high-alert state left him expecting a possible attack, where his body was overly tense from being on high alert. He would at times replay the mental movie in his mind for what he had witnessed, re-feeling the negative and uncomfortable emotions that he experienced physically from the trauma he watched in his mind. He found it easy to lock himself away from the world, crowded spaces and social gatherings, as he felt comfortable at home, even though he was still on edge in his own body. There were times where he could function with ease, working, socializing, exercising, and enjoying life, but in the back of his mind he would always be on alert for his surroundings, feeling a level of anxiety for any possible threats.

As the incident had happened years before our work started, he described how he felt he had changed from being an outgoing person to a less confident person who would sometimes "be" like his former self, but then get pulled back into the feelings of anxiety. This had shaped how he interacted with people, the choices he made, how he communicated and worked, and it even disrupted his sleep patterns. As there were some days or even weeks where it was easy for him to live his day-to-day life, he felt that the feelings and experience had become more distant, but then they would come back stronger, more overpowering and, in some ways, as he reflected, almost like a call from within for help.

HOW TO HEAL

One of the most powerful therapeutic methods that I have come across, which I pretty much use in every coaching session I do, is Integral Eye Movement Therapy (IEMT). Similar but also in many ways different to EMDR, IEMT can offer possible immediate relief from the feelings and experience of trauma. I have worked with people who have experienced sexual abuse, domestic violence, accidents and natural disasters and this process can desensitize and even eliminate the overpowering feelings and emotions of the past events that can often be re-lived in the mind. Releasing these past experiences can also have a huge reduction in the present-day anxiety a person feels.

OBSESSIVE COMPULSIVE DISORDER (OCD)

There are various types of OCD, and each person will fall on to an individual spectrum for where their OCD falls for the area they are compulsively obsessive. OCD could be looked at as learned behaviour, but also a compulsion that is developed over time or quite immediately from a response to anxiety that acts as a distraction from the feeling and experience of being anxious. Usually, the individual will be searching internally to get to a point of either control, safety, satisfaction or acceptance within themselves for the area that they have obsessive compulsive behaviour for.

An individual may have obsessive thoughts that they feel that they cannot control or escape from where they often ruminate mentally through a variety of thoughts, obsessing over a situation in their life. They can feel more anxious if the situation is future based and out of their control; however, they can also fixate on situations from the past obsessively. These thought patterns, which can often be intrusive and feel as though they are involuntarily taking over the individual's attention and focus, can lead to intense feelings and emotions of anxiety. In other areas an individual may perform or engage in a behaviour that they feel an overwhelming compulsion to carry out, which depending on the individual may be a distraction or coping mechanism from the anxiety that they feel and experience within.

OCD MINDSET

Here the person is rarely present. They can be engaged in an activity, yet mentally thinking through their obsessive thoughts with regards to something that they cannot control in their life, or something they feel they need to get in control. There will probably be a lot of inner dialogue with a fast-speaking inner voice that feels uncontrollable. Their mind may be organized for the number of times they say something to themselves, where they think over a number of situations or scenarios repeatedly until they feel a sense of ease to end the cycle of thinking.

CASE STUDY

Bethany needed to clean the house from top to bottom at the start of each day as soon as the kids were out of the house. She had a cleaner come three times a week, but she would always shadow her, cleaning behind her as she moved through the home. Together we figured out that the obsessive cleaning was in fact a distraction tactic, and she was really feeling anxiety about her young children not being in her care while they were at school. She feared something would go wrong while they were outside the home, and so to occupy herself she would clean intensely in order to distract herself from the intrusive thoughts that bombarded her mind. She needed to feel anything other than the feelings of anxiety, which often got so bad they left her feeling nauseous. As she cleaned, she counted each job, heading back to job one, then job two and so on, mentally counting her way through each completed task and ahead to the jobs to do, so that her inner voice had a focus beyond fear.

HOW TO HEAL

Usually, OCD can leave you feeling uptight and tense, stressed and always on the move. Effective slow, deep breathing can help you to relax mentally, emotionally and physically. As you breathe and relax your body, you can also spend time working on your thought processes in terms of the mental movies and thoughts that are causing you to feel anxious, as well as the inner voice that you hear inside your head. Developing a more calming, reassured and less anxious inner voice can go a long way in quickly changing the way that your mind is operating and then causing you to feel. Consider specifically focusing on the area of your life that may be causing you to feel anxious, which you may be distracting yourself from through your OCD to help relieve the overpowering feelings of anxiety that contribute to your obsessive behaviour. More details on developing these skills is found in the self-action section.

BODY DYSMORPHIC DISORDER (BDD)

In some ways similar to OCD, the individual can focus on areas of their physical appearance where they feel either they are flawed, lacking in perfection, wanting to improve or even enhance or change. The anxiety experienced can be different for each individual and they can often feel anxious in relation to a body-related issue. They may often worry about their appearance, how others see them, how their physical shape appears and may frequently monitor their body weight. There may be days or individual times where they feel at ease with their body-focused area that they have been fixating on, and other times where they feel emotionally overwhelmed from the disappointment, they feel that can lead into anxiety. BDD can impact not only your self-esteem, but your social life, professional engagements and interactions and it can even contribute to social anxiety. You may find yourself comparing your physical body to past photos of yourself, other people, people online that you do not know and generally always be analysing aspects of your appearance. The emotional rollercoaster that you go on can leave you feeling angry with yourself, others and situations quite quickly; you may feel emotionally low and even depressed at times.

BDD MINDSET

The Individual may at times find themselves overthinking with regards to their appearance. This may happen whilst looking in the mirror or even at current or past photographs of themselves. During an anxious episode they may feel emotionally low as they are nit-picking and being overly critical of a particular area of their body or their entire appearance. They may lack confidence and no matter how well you tell them that they look, it comes down to what they say to themselves with their inner voice and their thoughts which will lead them to feel a sense of acceptance or further into anxiety to continue their obsession on their appearance. With BDD the individual may go from one extreme to the other with relation to the food that they eat and their self-discipline around their diet. They may also avoid social circles, feel let down if others do not notice or comment on their physical gains or losses, and fall into a cycle where they believe they need to work out more or adjust their diet to enhance their results.

CASE STUDY

Over the years I have worked with various people from the media. Professionally, a lot of them have modelled for different brands, from photographic to catwalk modelling. What has surprised me is the lack of confidence so many have expressed to me in their sessions and also the continual pattern of being overly self-critical. Most of the issues come from labelling themselves as "lacking in confidence". As we move from this surface level description of their personal challenges and into a more detailed exploration of their personal world, it becomes clear that there are issues of BDD. Taking away the pressure of the industry that they are in, to look good, to be well presented and to be fashion forward, it always surprises me how many individuals within this industry, an industry that so many strive to be a part of, have an overly active inner critic. Moving from a "lack of confidence" the communication becomes more open and more personal as they go on to describe how they fixate on an area of their body or their appearance that they feel dissatisfied with. I have heard from many how they overly exercise to be a particular shape or build. How others frequently have cosmetic procedures, weekly tanning top-ups and even weekly haircuts. They may then fixate and criticize the area of their appearance that they have "worked on", including staring at themselves in the mirror, watching back film footage of themselves and going over media photos for how they have appeared. Comparison plays a big part of their emotional discomfort. They will often compare elements of their physical body and appearance to other people online or that they know, which feeds the fixation and low self-esteem that leaves them feeling stuck in a cycle of feeling emotionally low.

HOW TO HEAL

Consider working with a BDD experienced professional who can help you to facilitate a wider understanding and change of thoughts where necessary to explore the areas that you may identify that cause you any anxiety.

PERINATAL ANXIETY

Anxiety can be experienced through different stages of pregnancy or even within the first few years of raising a newborn. Postpartum depression is often spoken about and sometimes even experienced by fathers not just mothers within the first year of being a parent. Perinatal anxiety can, however, be experienced from becoming pregnant, during the pregnancy period, before labour or after the child is born, usually over the first year of the child's life. Women may have anxiety around carrying the child during the months they are pregnant or feel anxious about giving birth. Once the baby has arrived, the anxiety may be directed towards the health and wellbeing of the child, where the mother feels overly anxious for the responsibility of the welfare for the newborn child. The anxiety may grow into feeling anxious about taking the child out into the local community. Travelling with the child may become an issue, as can having people around the child as the mother may feel overwhelmed by external sources that may not be clean enough for the mother's liking or may pose a threat to the baby's health.

PERINATAL ANXIETY MINDSET

Time spent overthinking during pregnancy can be triggered by various things including the impending due date, the life changes to the adults that lie ahead, feeling unprepared mentally and emotionally to raise a child and also the added responsibilities that will soon be a part of the adult's life. An individual who has had difficulty conceiving or who may have unfortunately experienced miscarriage may also feel overly anxious during the pregnancy period. The mother to be can feel on edge, overly in touch with her body, where she panics, assesses and questions any discomfort, and generally feels on edge through each trimester.

After the labour the mother may spend most of her time with the baby and may be reluctant to let the baby be alone without her presence. The mother may feel that she needs to have eyes on the baby at all times. If she is not holding the baby, she will want to be able to see or hear the baby to feel a sense of ease. The mother is likely to overthink situations regarding the child's safety and may obsessively check on the child when sleeping or fixate on the amount of feeding that is complete as well as the amount of physical bonding that is endured between baby and mother. Whilst out and about the mother may feel overwhelmed with people around that may pose a possible threat to the baby and may even restrict herself for how far she goes in terms of distance from the comfort of her home.

CASE STUDY

Laura became anxious as her baby bump started to get bigger. The reality of what was growing, not only inside her but into her actual life, made her feel as if she wasn't prepared for what life changes lay ahead. The lack of knowledge she felt she had, which really was the need to be prepared and in control, left her feeling overly anxious, and the anxiety grew as she got closer to her delivery date. Laura felt overwhelmed by the lack of control she had over the labour too, which could go in any direction.

Anna had felt completely grounded and calm during her pregnancy, and so her experience of anxiety came out of nowhere. At times she struggled when she was not in the company of her newborn, and even when walking her daughter in the local area she had known all of her life, she feared the worst and constantly felt on edge, imagining all the potential threats to her child, which made leaving the house very difficult.

For both Anna and Laura their anxiety had grown and continued to grow from becoming pregnant to now being mothers. Both had not experienced anxiety before and it was the responsibility of their children, the changes and adjustments to their living, and the anxiety of separation that left them feeling anxious.

HOW TO HEAL

Feeling reassured about your child is always going to determine whether you're anxious or relaxed. The key is to use your inner voice to change and reframe your thoughts when you may feel anxious about your baby. Look for certainty, reassure yourself with your inner voice and learn in small steps to have time away from your child. In the anticipation of labour, learn to breathe and to feel relaxed, (breathing methods are available in the self-action section) as this skill can change and transform how you feel post-labour.

*　*　*

Whether you feel you fit into a box from any of the above definitions, my advice is to allow yourself to get to working on your thoughts and feelings in relation to your anxiety. Instead of feeling limited in your thinking and defined by a "disorder", consider how you can engage your mind through your thoughts to transform how you are feeling, which will allow you to get to a point where you begin to take more control over your anxiety. Through effort, focus and determination, you can transform your experience of anxiety and have more input into the way in which your mind works, which will in turn improve how your body is feeling.

PERSONAL GPS

Take a moment to practise, to shift, to feel and direct your awareness to being freely in the present moment. Look past these words and for a few minutes, see, hear and feel the space and place around. Be present. See, hear and feel.

THE ROAD
TO FREEDOM

Endless paths are tiring to walk.

Hills often take your breath away.

The horizon may seem far, but the journey is worth taking.

WHAT'S IN YOUR MIND
IS IN YOUR BODY

One of the major themes of NLP that we touched on earlier in the book is the mind–body connection. For many years, various individuals considered the mind to be separate from the body. This we now know is definitely not the case. There is a constant flow of communication between the mind and the thoughts that are being formed, as well as the body to the brain, through feelings, emotions and even physical sensations and symptoms. **What you think, you will feel.**

As you think through your very many thousands of daily thoughts, from what you imagine and see in your mind, to what you say and hear with your inner voice, your body will be carrying the experience of your thoughts physically and emotionally. The thoughts that you think will be transported by electrical impulses along neurons, where neurotransmitters connect through synaptic gaps which carry and transfer electric impulses throughout the body. Thought after thought, bridges begin to build and connect pathways that carry and produce the feelings and emotions that you feel physically throughout your body. If your thoughts continue to consider anxiety-inducing scenarios or situations, then the feelings that will flow physically and quite easily will be the many feelings of anxiety that can accelerate and grow with ease. It's the same for happiness, joy, gratitude, desire and excitement. What you think in your mind will always flow into your body, as thoughts create feelings. The power here lies in your understanding that your mind can and will create the physical experience in your body. This means you can consciously create the feelings in your body that you want to feel, which leaves you in a powerful position.

It's very easy for me to suggest changing the channel of thoughts in your mind, or the narrative of fear and anxiety that you often hear, but if you do, then you will get an entirely different physical experience, which could be for the better. It can be that simple, powerfully simple if it is better for you to think of it that way. In taking clients through the process to **see**, **hear**, and **feel** their current environment, they will often communicate to me that they feel calm, immediately relaxed, and free from any difficult thoughts. This is because the process not only helps to direct the awareness of your mind, which increases your focus and leaves you quickly arriving into the present moment alongside your physical body with great ease, but it allows you to feel the ease physically not just mentally. If you watch a horror movie on Netflix, you will feel the physical sensations in your body from what you see and hear. It is the same in your mind. What you see and hear in the space and place of your thoughts is always going to influence the feelings and emotions in your body.

- How often do you pay attention to your thoughts and how those thoughts are creating the feelings and emotions that you are feeling in your body?
- How often do you pay attention to the physical sensations, symptoms and even possible challenges that

your body is presenting to you, trying to communicate to your awareness that something needs addressing?

What you think you will feel. – Yes, I am repeating myself because repetition allows you to be reminded that this simple formula, mantra or reminder can help you to interrupt the feelings of anxiety by directing your awareness to your thoughts. You may often feel and experience the very many different feelings of anxiety that could be panic, fear, stress, worry, nerves, sadness, feeling uncertain and even on edge, which can be a clear instigator to check in with your mind and your thoughts. The physical sensations that you feel, whether it's churning in your gut, jelly in your legs, a weight on your shoulders or a general whole-body freeze, can be physical communication for you to focus on your thoughts. In changing your thoughts, the way that you are thinking, from what you see in your mind and hear yourself saying, you can immediately change the physical experiences in your body. It's not just the brain and your thoughts that communicates to your body through producing physical experiences, it is the body talking back and even calling out to the mind.

A few years ago, I had experienced various gut challenges where my body, through the physical struggles and challenges that were experienced in my digestive system, attempted again and again to grab my attention. I lived with them for nearly two years, bloated, constipated and frustrated with the physical challenges that seemed to slowly get worse over time. It was easy for me to ignore them, but my body struggled to cope and eventually got my attention for a call to action where I consulted a nutritionist. Following the guidance and specific plan for my symptoms, I was amazed at the changes that began to physically happen within 48 hours of me following the advice of my practitioner. If I had literally listened to my gut a lot sooner, I could have eased and even prevented the symptoms that I experienced by answering the call from within that my body kept on calling out to me.

This in many ways is the same for your anxious feelings that will be calling out for you to find some healing and inner peace. You may have probably experienced that the longer you have left your anxiety untreated, the stronger it has become in its desire to get your attention. Think of it this way, that your anxiety is calling you, asking you, and even telling you that something inside of you needs addressing. The way that your body can attempt time after time to communicate with you that something needs your attention is perhaps a new way for you to consider in working through the challenging feelings and emotions that you are experiencing within. I have worked with people who have gut challenges, skin conditions, panic and anxiety attacks, severe stress and burnout, which all have a variety of physical symptoms that are a loop of mind talking to the body and, in many ways, the body expressing the state of the mind. **What you think you will feel.**

Let's experience the mind–body connection now with some exercises that allow you to change how you feel by changing your thought patterns.

ANCHORING

Recalling past memories with positive states is known as "anchoring" in NLP, and I use this technique quite often to help people quickly shift their mental and emotional state.

Let's try it now:

1. Bring to mind a specific time with family or friends where you were laughing uncontrollably and feeling happy.
2. Take a moment, think back and now bring it to your awareness.
3. Hear the laughter and notice the positive shift it creates in your body.
4. Close your eyes and picture the memory. See it in your mind, hear the sounds and feel the shift in how you feel.
5. Label this memory (example "fun time with family") so that you can recall it quickly anytime you want to feel these feelings. The more often you think of it, the stronger the feelings that you'll feel.

As you may have just experienced to some degree, you can direct the focus of your thoughts and transform the feelings and emotions in your body from what you're choosing to focus on. This is helpful, because you can't feel anxiety when you're feeling joy. You can't feel anxious when you're feeling grateful. In changing your thoughts, you can change how you feel, and quickly.

Use the prompts below to come up with a bank of past memories to recall when you need help to shift your focus away from your anxious feelings to then access more resourceful states.

1. Think of two places where you feel safe, calm or relaxed.
2. Think of two places where you feel the environment is peaceful.
3. Think of two specific times when you were really laughing.
4. Think of two specific times when you felt happy and content.

Now use the previous steps 1–5 on the previous page each with two examples you have just listed, where you label each example, to anchor and access the desired emotional state.

From the pictures that you see, the mental movies that you watch, the inner sounds you hear and converse with, these elements of your thinking all contribute to your emotional experience both positively and negatively. Now you can actively create more calming, reassuring, positive and empowering pictures and sounds with your thoughts so that you can dissolve any feelings of anxiety.

EXERCISE: SHIFTING STATES METHOD

1. Use an example from your list or think now about a place that you have been where you felt calm and relaxed. It could be on a beach, a walk in nature, lying in the sun in your back garden or looking out across the horizon from a hill or mountain.

    a. *Visual option*: See the space in your mind. Mentally walk in the environment as if you are there. Hear the sounds and feel the calm throughout your body. Do this for 60 seconds.

    b. *Auditory option*: Listen to your inner voice describing the calm, relaxed place that you now remember. Discuss how it made you feel with your inner voice in great detail to evoke the experience. Do this for 60 seconds.

2. In spending some time with this past memory, notice how you begin to feel in your body now that you have shifted your awareness to this calm space.

3. Use your inner voice to communicate what you currently need. Firstly, identify what you want to feel. Is it calm, reassured, relaxed, present or perhaps confident? Having identified your chosen state, switch it on in your body by using your inner voice to speak in the space inside your head. "I am calm", "I choose to relax", "I now choose to be present". Instead of being pulled back and forth from

your thoughts, allow your inner voice to direct you to feeling more ease within, as you actively use your mind to interrupt any anxious thoughts.

4. Shift your inner GPS to the present space that you are in and stop going ahead into "what if" situations with your thoughts. Look, listen and feel into your awareness of your present space to shift from being internal with your thoughts, to being external with the ease and freedom that's outside of you.

Whether you changed your emotional state by thinking about a calm or relaxed place or whether you felt more positive or happier from previously thinking back to a time with loved ones, acknowledge the change in how you felt. It's important to notice the shifts in how you felt.

TIME-TRAVELLING
THOUGHTS

Exit the cave of fear and walk away from the cliff edge of
worry. Instead choose to walk the beach of solitude or sit
at the lake of peace in the spaces and places that you visit
in your mind. They're only thoughts, but they are there for
you to mentally exist in. Choose your inner environments
wisely and feel the waterfalls of self-care flow calmly within.

TAKING THE OUTSIDE IN AND EXPERIENCING THE INSIDE OUT

In every environment that you're in, you will be unconsciously taking in elements of your surroundings through your senses. You are most likely unaware of how you receive each moment, and you probably pay little attention to it, as it happens so naturally for you. Without thinking about it, you will use your eyes to see, ears to hear, your sense of touch to feel, and may also consider aspects of smell and tastes to some degree.

This is the basis of the NLP communication model, which highlights how our senses formulate our individual subjective experiences. The model suggests that our brains naturally filter our experiences so that we can digest, interpret and comfortably handle our sensory experiences through simmering down and filtering each second of each moment, which happens naturally for us. Through the process of filtering, you will automatically delete, distort and generalize each place and space from the millions of bits of data and information that surround you to a smaller level that is easier for you to process.

This could be anywhere from 2 million bits of data in each place and each space per second, which is filtered down to somewhere around 134 bits of data, though this figure is only a guide and is constantly being revised. To understand it further, imagine if you can 2 million different chocolates floating through the air around you, above, below and to each side, and reproducing that same number of new chocolates each and every second. As you consider that very high number of chocolates, consider being able to reach out and grab only two handfuls per second. These two handfuls are what you are left with in your experience from the total number of chocolates. In the same way, your senses will "grab" your two handfuls of each moment and filter out the rest, by deleting, distorting and generalizing them.

DELETION

Filtering your experiences happens naturally on an unconscious level. This is because there is far too much information to take in and process each second, for every second of each place and space that you are in. As you are reading this section now, you are probably not consciously aware of the feeling of the fabric of your clothing as it touches different parts of your skin. You may now to some degree start to sense and feel this as I have brought it to your attention. You may not be consciously thinking how you need to breathe, where you need to actively direct each inhale and exhale, as it happens without you having to think about your breathing. You may now to some degree again start to become more aware as you are reading this, of the flow and movement and perhaps even the sound of your breath as you continue to read. You most probably were not aware of the position and feeling of your tongue touching the back of your teeth as it rests in your mouth until now. How does that now feel as I've now brought it to your awareness?

These are examples of how elements of our experiences are naturally filtered through "deletion" from our conscious awareness. This process of deletion will filter information through ways that it has been wired over time to best serve you. You couldn't possibly be aware of every sound in the room that you're in, while simultaneously aware of every function that your organs are performing, while visually aware of every piece of furniture in the room. Deletion is a normal and natural process that allows you to not feel overwhelmed by the sheer amount of data available to us. Without the ability to delete, you would simply feel overwhelmed and exhausted; it's also a process which differs from person to person in relation to what specifically is being deleted.

If you are walking through an art gallery with a good friend, you may later be sat having a coffee talking about the experience of being in the gallery and you may recall a very different experience to the one your friend describes. This is simply because your focus of attention will be different to theirs and to what you have naturally deleted and focused upon whilst in the gallery. You could be having a conversation with one person in a room filled with over 100 people, but you naturally filter out the background noise without thinking, to be able to hear the person you are talking with. Deletion happens naturally all of the time. One person walking down the street may hear the sounds of the birds, and to another, the view of the trees may be their choice of focus. Deletion helps you to not feel overwhelmed, although the feeling of anxiety may in fact be leading you to feel completely overwhelmed.

When anxious, it is quite common that you may filter out and delete elements of safety, certainty and reassurance that are actually around you, in your present moment and a true part of your reality. With some of the people I have worked with they have gotten into a habit of deleting the good elements in their life, aspects of safety, positive attributes about themselves, as they tend to focus more on the negative, more challenging and uncertain aspects of their experience.

Bringing their focus more consciously back to the positive areas that they can feel certain over, which leaves them feeling in control and safe, has allowed them to expand their deletion filter to not overly focus on the difficult parts of their experience.

Consider for yourself:

- What could you be deleting from your experience that is causing you to focus on the feeling and possible threat of anxiety?
- As you naturally delete data from space to space, getting an idea of where your focus is can enlighten you in many ways for how you may be thinking. Is your focus on an area of your life that then leads you to feel anxious?
- Are you deleting the ease of the present moment?
- Could you be missing out on the freedom of being in the now by mentally venturing out into the future with your thoughts?

In becoming aware of how you are thinking, you can begin to take ownership of how you are feeling. Think of it this way: would you spend half of your day sat staring at a fence, turning your back on the most beautiful garden? Would you choose to focus on the darkest, grimmest part when you could be experiencing the beauty of the colours, the feeling of the grass and the sounds of the birds that may surround you? Where your focus is directed is always going to influence the way that you feel. Fence or garden? Anxiety or peace? The key is to become aware of what you may be deleting from the ease and simplicity of the present moment, and where you may be automatically focusing your attention through your thoughts on areas of your life that may be producing the experience of anxiety within your body.

EXERCISE

Write a list of 10 experiences – from today or from this week or last month – that were not ones of anxiety.

For example, "I felt safe and in control taking the kids to school" or "I watched TV at home without feeling anxious."

By writing down and highlighting the times you were not anxious, you are bringing awareness to the moments of ease and control in your day-to-day life that can naturally get deleted from your usual focus on anxiety. As a result, you can start to expand the filters of your mind. Making lists like this daily can help train your mind to live beyond what it perceives as only anxious experiences.

GENERALIZATION

Another aspect that forms your reality within each moment is the NLP filter known as generalization. You will naturally receive without analysing language that is communicated to you – from the words that you speak to the words that you hear, as you do not think consciously about each and every sentence spoken to you. Over time, your understanding becomes unconscious. You are not having to think deeply about each word that you are reading. Your learning of language from your early education and over time each and every day has allowed you to understand people that communicate the languages that you understand with great ease. It is the same with each element that you are taking in through your sensory experience, each and every second. You are not holding this book or reading device re-learning that this is a book or e-reader. You are not experiencing each door that you walk through in your home or place of work as a new experience. Very quickly you will have learnt what a door is and how it works, so that you do not have to re-learn and teach yourself every time you come across one.

The process of generalizing happens quite quickly and can have positive aspects: for example, not having to learn every single time you open a door that this is now a door, as life would be slow and overly boring. There can also be negative generalizations that individuals make, including things like, all builders are cowboys. Another extreme example could be all teenagers drink and take drugs. Any single individual experience may lead to a negative generalization where an area of focused attention can lead to a conclusion, which may in some respects be quite limiting for how you live and then generalize aspects of your life.

With anxiety you could in many ways have had an experience which then generalizes into the possible threat of a future experience that causes you to presently feel anxious. For example, a business partnership that you may have trusted which led to you being manipulated and taken advantage of, may lead you to feel anxious about working with other people as you progress with your business or career. An unfortunate relationship challenge where your partner betrays your trust may then cause you to naturally assume that your next partner having moved on with your relationship and at a completely different time in your life, may leave you feeling anxious with regards to trusting your new and perfectly stable relationship. One past experience where you may have felt intimidated or anxious from walking past a group of people, may generalize to feel anxiety at other similar times. Generalizing that all groups on all streets may offer a potential threat can affect the way that you feel, the way that you work and interact with people and also leave you confined to the walls of your home, through the anxiety and fear of being out and about. One experience doesn't have to lead to a lifetime of thinking and feeling in a particular way. The challenge may be in breaking the current cycle of generalized anxious thinking as there is no need to feel a sense of anxiety for possible similar future experiences.

Consider for yourself:

- Could your anxiety be part of a generalized experience that you have come to conclude as your reality?
- Do you know of any situations in your life or in the life of those that you know where your anxiety doesn't exist?
- Is your belief around the area that's causing you anxiety generally limiting you from being present and feeling at ease on a daily basis?
- How long have you had this belief and what was the experience that caused you to know this to now be true in your reality and in your future?

EXERCISE

Make a list of any generalizations that you believe may be a cause of your anxiety, and where possible your filter of generalizing has been incorrect.

For example: "I thought every relationship was going to be challenging *but I am surprised at how easy it is to get along with my partner.*"

Or: "I had been anxious about moving house as something always goes wrong, *but this time everything went smoothly, which was refreshing.*"

DISTORTION

Our final area of NLP filtering for you to consider is known as distortion. This is where you have the ability to construct, formulate and imagine situations and scenarios that are not yet in your present reality. The mind's ability to go back in time to think through past situations, as well as to think ahead to the possibilities of the future, can lead to positive and negative feelings and emotions that are experienced within the present moment. As your senses receive the various data of your surroundings, you may at times distort what you see, hear or feel to then contribute to the feelings of anxiety. An example of an easily made distortion that I have found myself experiencing a few times is where I have seen a rope in the street or even a long branch when walking through the woods and perceived both of them as a snake. This short glimpse of what I believed to be in front of me is a distortion of what I believed I had seen. My mind believed even for a short moment that a snake was in fact there, leading me to feel immediately fearful. I quickly realized what I believed I had seen was not true.

Where I've seen anxiety presented through distortion with some of the people that I have worked with, is the distorted reality and experience that life around them is a constant threat. Their perception of leaving their home, going to work and being in the company of certain people at work has become distorted, for the belief that they perceive to be true, and for some reason it now causes them to be in a state of anxiety. I have also worked with people suffering relationship anxiety where they believed that their partner was cheating on them, which led them to see every action their partner did was in some ways part of them living and acting behind their back, again causing them to feel anxious. The result of feeling overly anxious for two months and the perception and belief of their partner's behaviour brought overwhelming shock and emotion when they were proposed to, as the feeling of regret overwhelmed their happiness in the proposal for their distorted belief of an affair was suddenly realized as far from the truth.

Consider for yourself:

- Could your anxiety be a result of your thoughts distorting aspects of your reality?
- From social anxiety to travel anxiety, what are you thinking or saying to yourself that is causing you to feel anxious about a certain situation or experience in your life?
- How specifically do I know this to be true?
- What is my evidence that this is a true cause for my anxiety? Or could it be something that I have come to believe from what I have allowed myself to think?

Have you ever feared something would happen and then it never did? I'd hazard a guess that 95 per cent of what you consider and construct in your mind when you're experiencing anxious thoughts never actually occurs. Use the following exercise to identify instances of distorted thinking.

EXERCISE

Make a list of the times you thought something that caused you to have anxious feelings, but then had a totally different experience.

For example: "I thought friends are all talking about me behind my back, but the last three times I've seen my friends, it's clear that they are not even thinking about me behind my back let alone talking about me."

Or: "I thought my housemate was annoyed with me and had convinced myself of it for days, but it turned out they were not annoyed at all, and they just wanted some alone time."

The key here is to find the evidence that leads you to think, feel and realize that you had constructed your thoughts. Shifting your thinking and most importantly your feelings from the distorted to the certain reality can help disrupt anxious thought patterns. In listing the areas that you considered possible sources of anxiety but were then proven wrong, you can expand the filters of your mind beyond any limiting distortions.

The filtering process of deletion, distortion and generalization will leave you with an internal representation that you see or hear within your thoughts. This can be pictures or mental movies, inner sounds or a combination of them together. This will be formulated and influenced by the external elements of what's around you but also internal factors, including the way you perceive a situation within your thoughts. Whether its deletion, distortion or generalization that is leading you to focus on and experience anxiety, the key is to improve the way your mind is thinking for the way you may be filtering your individual experiences. This is all part of developing your mindset, which will require practice, perseverance and patience as you begin to expand your filters beyond the anxious ways of thinking that may have become automatically habitual for you.

A daily list can go a long way in helping you expand the filters of your mind where you may naturally be deleting, distorting and generalizing aspects of ease and focusing on being anxious. Take your time to write, feel and connect with your thoughts to help your mind expand to encompass all the good and ease that may well be happening in your life without you noticing it. In bringing any aspect of certainty, safety or feeling in control into your awareness, you can naturally form new habits of thinking where your mind will pick up and focus on these positive areas instead of only "seeing", "feeling" and "experiencing" anxiety.

ON TRIAL

The evidence suggests that there are far too many examples that detail times of feeling free, calm, in control, at ease and not being anxious. It is your job to remind the anxiety that is accused that the evidence outweighs the claims that any anxiety offers. The claims made by anxiety are simply over-exaggerated constructions of the mind. The truth is carried by various examples and should be seriously taken into consideration as you determine your verdict on the anxiety that is in question.

HOW YOUR THOUGHTS ARE FORMED

As your mind naturally deletes, distorts and generalizes each subjective experience that you have, you will be left with specific internal representations that you then hold in your mind. It always amazes me how the people I work with become fascinated with how their mind operates and forms their internal representations. From highly educated lawyers, nurses who have had years of training and education, to teachers: finding out about their thoughts is like opening the instructions manual to the mind. I've worked with teenagers to 70-year-olds who have all felt oddly confused, inspired and even enlightened (all feelings that are not anxiety!) in gaining an understanding of their thoughts and how they are formed.

From an NLP perspective, you can now begin to understand elements of your **preferred representational** system for how you are encoding and giving meaning to your internal representations. A preferred representational system looks at how you may be formulating and structuring your thoughts, how you take in your personal experiences and translate them internally through your senses.

Would you consider yourself as a "visual thinker"?

The thoughts that you think, which are formulated and experienced inside your head, may appear as still images or pictures, mental movies, or scenes that you watch play out, or at times even feature in. These pictures or movies may be of the past or future, or thoughts formulated through images relating to anxiety in the present moment. You may be more visual with your thinking, whether it's for the past or thoughts for the future. It can also vary on the context you are thinking about and the area that you are experiencing as to whether your thoughts will be formulated in visual form.

If you are a visual thinker, I'm sure that you can now think of a past wedding, birthday or recent celebration. As it draws you back to that past time, spend a moment to notice how it's presented and accessed in picture form in your mind.

- Is it a mental movie or still image?
- Is it vivid and clear or hard to recall?
- Notice how it makes you feel and where you feel those feelings in your body.

You may also be aware of the thoughts that you think repetitively in picture or movie form in relation to the future that leaves you feeling anxious, that you often spend time thinking through. A lot of people I work with naturally communicate: "I keep watching the worst possible things happening over and over in my head, which leaves me feeling anxious." Whether it's the past or future that you think of, can you notice if elements of your thinking are formed through visual aspects? Not everyone is visual with their thoughts, and you can vary to what degree your visual thoughts appear within your mind. Being visual through pictures and mental movies may be something that formulates your thought processes that you may now be able to reflect upon and notice.

This increased awareness for how you are thinking is important. It's also important to note that the way that your mind operates can vary with each experience, the company that you are in and for where you currently are. At times you may be more visual with your thoughts, and in others you may hear more sounds and inner dialogue inside your head.

Would you consider yourself as an "auditory thinker"?

The second aspect of your thinking to consider is the collective of inner sounds that may formulate the way that you're thinking about your anxiety. As you think through and explore your thoughts you may be able to identify that you have your inner voices or at times various inner dialogues? For some individuals thinking through inner discussion, talking through their thoughts, and thinking ahead through inner voice discussion is how they structure their thinking. These people will be more in tune with the sounds and words of their experiences and perhaps less visual in their thoughts. This is the "auditory thinker". In relation to your inner sounds, there are usually a variety of voices that you will communicate with, perhaps you have noticed some of them? There may be one dominant voice with a particular tone, volume and speed that it communicates with that you can recognize. There may be other people's voices – for example, a parent, colleague, teacher or even a partner that you hear talking inside your own head through your thoughts. The sounds that you hear from the thoughts that you think, whether you're engaging with inner talk, or even feeling that you can't stop the voice of anxiety, are all going to influence your present mental and emotional state. Quite often I ask individuals if they would openly talk out aloud the things they hear inside their head or the things that they say to themselves. The answer is usually no. Words can have so much power. Words spoken with your inner voice can not only powerfully influence your emotions, but they can shape your behaviour and the results that you get in your life. Perhaps you can identify if your thoughts are formulated through sounds rather than pictures?

Would you consider yourself as a "combination thinker"?

The experiences that you have through the sounds of your thoughts can at times also be a combination of pictures and sounds that are formulating your internal experience. This is the third aspect of your thinking to now consider, pictures with sounds. Perhaps you have a combination of both visual and sound like I tend to do?

Would you consider yourself as a "feelings-based thinker"?

Some people tend to feel more quickly, which is the final area to consider in relation to how you think and also feel. You may often be aware of the feelings and where you feel them in your body, and not so aware of the images and sounds that are causing those feelings to exist in your emotional body. These feelings may take your focus and draw your energy to where you feel the anxiety in your body, which could cause you to be overpowered by the feelings of anxiety, where you struggle to direct your focus to your thoughts. The power lies in identifying and working with your thoughts to action, **"what you think you will feel"**, to override the disempowering feelings of anxiety.

Your thoughts may happen at speeds that feel as though they are hard to put a stop to. They may often feel that they have a power and strength of their own where you feel you have no control over what you see and what you hear inside your own head. You may now be able to identify if you're more visual or auditory based, or more combination based with how you experience your thoughts, or perhaps you tend to be more aware of your feelings and emotions rather than the pictures and the sounds you hear and see within your thoughts?

Still not quite sure? Let's try an exercise to help you identify what type of thinker you are:

- Think back to the last meal that you cooked and ate. When you have that memory, how is it formed and constructed inside your head? Did you see it, say it or hear it? Or did you feel a particular way first? Perhaps you even have elements of taste or smell coming to mind?

- Now think back to a conversation you were having with a friend recently. When you have that memory, how is it formed and constructed inside your head? Did you see it, say it or hear it? Or did you feel a particular way first?

- Think about going to work next week. As you step into those thoughts, notice how it is it formed and constructed inside your head. Did you see it, say it or hear it? Or did you feel a particular way first?

Considering your responses to the above, if you saw a picture in your head, you may be more visual. If you heard yourself, you may be more auditory based. If you recalled and felt a feeling, you may be more in tune with your emotions.

As you get to understand the many components of your mindset, this can help lead you to understand how your anxiety is being structured and formulated from what you're thinking, which is leading you to then feel anxious.

- When you think ahead to seeing a person you know, a family member or friend that you may be seeing in the next week or so, how is that structured in your mind? Are you seeing it? A still image or mental movie? Are you saying and hearing it? Having internal dialogue or conversation? Or are you more aware of how you feel?

- Perhaps consider a trip that you want to go on in the next six to twelve months. How does that experience formulate in your mind with your thoughts?

From pictures to sounds, movies to inner voices, you can get to understand what you are doing inside your head as you become more mindful of the way that your thoughts are formed and structured. This may all be new to you. Have you gotten this far in your life and not realized that you may have been overly watching all of the potential worst-case scenarios on the screen inside your head? Have there been times where you have heard that anxious inner voice talking fast, loud and overbearingly in a panic tone that has left you feeling tight and tense in your own body? I can pretty much accurately guess that a lot of the things that you've overly thought of have then never gone on to actually happen. They only lived in your mind with the feelings of anxiety that were felt in your body, disturbing your present moment, leaving you at times feeling helpless to escape from the internal grips of anxiety. Some of the situations and scenarios that you've thought of, watched and discussed in your head may have stopped you from living your life. This can be extremely draining mentally and emotionally. The need to be aware of how you are thinking is key for you to get a hold of your anxiety. It's through your awareness that you're going to be able to intervene quickly, to change the pattern of your thoughts that are only leaving you feeling anxious.

Everybody is different for how they think and with the structure and set up of their mind. You will experience your internal world differently to me. Your partner or best friend will think in a way that suits and works for them, as will the children in your life, as everybody has their own preferred representational system for how they encode and give meaning to their thoughts and reality. The type of thinker that you are can also change for the environment that you are in, the experience that you are having, as you may not be a fixed thinker and may naturally adapt and change from each situation. There will always be elements of either images, mental movies, inner voices and sounds. Some people will have a combination of all of these elements, and others will have only images with very little sounds, or total sounds with no images. Each mind and each person is different.

In considering how you are experiencing your anxiety, when you experience it, what causes it, and in getting a better understanding of what's happening inside your own head, you will be in a much better position to put your mind at ease.

I want you to now think about what you're specifically anxious about and then secondly identify how your thoughts are structuring your thinking in relation to your anxiety.

How to be more specific in understanding your subjective experience of anxiety:

Think of something specific you are anxious about.

Do you see any images?

- If so, are they pictures or mental movies?
- Are they in colour or black and white?
- What size are they?
- Are they clear and in focus or distorted and blurry?

Do you hear any sounds?

- If so, is it an inner voice?
- Is it a conversation?
- What's the volume on a scale of 1 to 10? (10 being the loudest)
- What speed are they running at? Fast or slow?

Now describe the feelings of anxiety:

- Where are they in your body?
- Are they moving or still?
- Strong or weak?
- Do they have a shape?

Once you have considered the ways in which you are thinking and feeling when anxious, you can begin to break down and transform the formulation of your anxious thoughts and put into practice the methods that I will give you in the next part of the book.

EXPANDING YOUR MAP
OF THE WORLD

If you walk the routes that are familiar that leave you feeling on edge, you live on edge. The key to your power is to expand the horizons of your mind for what you see and say to yourself, for a new world exists past the boundaries of your fears. A world of certainty, safety and security is accessible beyond the streets of anxiety that you continually walk.

Go there.

Think yourself to new places.

It all starts in your mind.

PART TWO

SELF-ACTION

This section will now cover various methods for the Anxiety Antidote that you can practise to help you relieve your anxiety. Utilizing the self-awareness that you have gained, you can now begin to "**self-action**" the tools and resources offered in this next part of the Anxiety Antidote to help you develop a deeper sense of self-control. Here I will offer examples and further information on anxiety in the context of each method to help you better understand the relationship you can now develop with your mind and emotions through your thoughts.

GATHER YOUR
EVIDENCE

There are various ways that anxiety can be experienced, from the mental to the physical symptoms, which can be different for each and every person. Some professionals and mental health organizations believe that certain criteria if met within your anxiety experience can lead to you possibly being diagnosed with an anxiety disorder. A "disorder" in my opinion sounds quite limiting. The word itself appears to me as a description of something that may be broken, out of sync and personally leaves the feeling or belief of being unchangeable, this is just my opinion.

Google dictionary defines the word "disorder" as "a state of confusion". I personally warm more to this definition, simply because through my personal experience of anxiety, along with my professional experience of working with people experiencing anxiety, I can identify anxiety as a mental and emotional "**state**". The good news here is that any emotional state can be changed and changed quite quickly. This can enable you to feel and experience that you are not stuck, you are not limited by a disorder, but you are simply and at times in an emotional state of anxiety.

Consider a toddler screaming and rolling around on the floor in a supermarket. The same toddler can be in a completely different emotional state when at the checkout, smiling, happy and even laughing. The toddler wouldn't stay stuck in the tantrum state for long periods of time. I believe that just as the emotional state of the toddler can be shifted, so can your anxious state, and framing anxiety in this way can enable you to feel that you are not stuck; you are simply, at times, in **an emotional state of anxiety**.

This is where we come back to my magic formula of "**what you think, you will feel**".

By controlling what you think, you can create order in your mind and body at any time, and in any place. This will help you to feel limitless and can be used along with the other tools and resources in this book, so that you can move forwards and transform your life for the better. By taking a position of being more open to creating more "order", let's consider dropping the "dis" and embracing the "order" that can be created and experienced in your life.

If you think about the times **when you are not anxious**, you have moved out of the **state** of anxiety. This could be when you're watching Netflix, sleeping, exercising, walking the dog, having a drink with a friend. At what other times in your life do you notice your anxiety resides? You may know all too well the times that your anxiety is there, present and overwhelming, but if you can identify times in the last week or even the previous day where you were not anxious, you may be able to notice where your emotional **state** shifts from anxiety to another emotional state. Gathering your evidence and actively writing out your examples of times that you are anxious can help expand the deletion, distortion and generalization filters of your mind. The evidence that you focus on daily can help weaken your mind's ability to focus on your anxious thoughts. You can even look back over the past days and weeks to help you realize and then generalize within your mindset the many times that you are not actually anxious, which will specifically help you expand your deletion filter.

EXERCISE: EVIDENCE LIST METHOD

1. Write out five times from today or yesterday or this week that you were not anxious.
2. List what you were doing, where you were and how you felt.
3. Read over the list and feel any emotional shifts as you realize and affirm any moments from your day, week or past where you have not been anxious. Continue your list on a daily basis with 5–10 examples each day.

Your **evidence list** is a great way to expand your mind in relation to your thinking and it can help you shift your anxious emotional state quickly as you gather your evidence. I suggest that you start your list which could be on your phone or writing it out in a notebook and create your evidence list once a day for 30 days. Aim to be consistent and write a daily list, as over the 30 days you will help expand the filters of your mindset. It may only take you a few minutes each day to formulate your list and you could read over the previous day to help your mind expand more rapidly as you visit and acknowledge the evidence in your day-to-day life for times that you are not anxious.

UNSUBSCRIBE

Your position in the overthinkers anxiety club is due for renewal. If you would like to continue to live stream the worse-case scenarios and listen regularly to your inner voice of anxiety, please take no immediate action to continue your VIP membership. To unsubscribe from the internal experience of anxiety, please instead choose **"self-action"** and integrate the Anxiety Antidote into your daily life.

REMOTE
CONTROL

Getting stuck in the space inside your head as you hear and discuss your thoughts or even watch the worst-case scenarios play out in your mind can feel very limiting. However, it is possible to shift your focus from the screen and sounds within by being more present with your GPS as you see, hear and feel your external environment.

Whether it's mental movies, still images or inner voices and sounds within your thoughts, it's time for you to now take the remote control to your mind and interrupt this disempowering cycle of anxious thinking. Interrupting the pattern can stop the flow of anxiety in your body and quickly. Stopping the pattern of thinking that is causing you to feel anxious will in many ways allow you to shift your position of thinking for the better, where you begin to actively take control over your thoughts.

EXERCISE:

REMOTE CONTROL METHOD

VISUAL THINKER OPTION

Stage 1

1. Identify how you are thinking. Do you have pictures or scenes in your thoughts?

2. Interrupt the pattern by pressing PAUSE on the mental movie you find yourself watching or freezing the image in your mind.

3. Try it now by thinking of any of your future-based thoughts that you may often think that cause you to feel anxious. See them play out in your mind and then press PAUSE on the thoughts to bring them to a standstill.

4. **Notice how it makes you feel** as you develop a sense of control and when the thoughts stop and pause in action.

Stage 2

5. Move the PAUSED visual thought away from you by making it go off into the distance.

6. Imagine you are swiping a screen and move it to the side, below you or even behind you so that it is completely out of sight.

7. Again, **feel and notice the difference** from interrupting the thought patterns, PAUSING them, and moving them out of sight.

Stage 3

8. Having interrupted the thought pattern, mindfully shift your awareness from your internal space to your present external space as you see, hear and feel the ease and freedom of the present moment as you align your mental and physical GPS.

AUDITORY THINKER OPTION

Stage 1

1. Identify how you are thinking. Do you hear internal sounds? Inner sounds/dialogue/inner chatter?

2. Hear the voice or sounds in your head that are formulating your anxiety.

3. Mentally **turn the volume on the sounds down** until they switch off.

4. Take your time and take your power by reducing the sounds down as quickly or slowly as you need as you would turn the sound down with a remote control.

5. Reduce the sound to very quiet or off completely. 10 being the loudest and 0 being silent.

6. Hear, notice, observe and enjoy the space of silence that now exists in your mind.

7. Repeat step 6 further to feel and experience the silence you have now actively created for 60 seconds.

8. Should the internal sounds return, repeat step 4 and have a more determined approach to make your inner space silent.

Stage 2

9. Having interrupted the thought pattern, mindfully shift your awareness from your internal space to your present external space as you see, hear and feel the ease and freedom of the present moment as you align your mental and physical GPS.

In utilizing these methods to take control of the thoughts that cause you to feel anxious, you can take back control over the state of your mind and emotions. The key is to actively interrupt the thought patterns to take their power away and actively use the remote control for your mind.

Practise either the visual option or the auditory option for 30 days in order to develop this skill, fully understand the process and to feel the shifts. Aim to be consistent and interrupt the anxious thought patterns as they occur, and then shift to being more present with your **Personal GPS**.

REALITY CHECK

If you see something on TV that is uncomfortable to watch, you simply change the channel. When you accidently slip and fall, you become more aware and cautious of your steps. If you're driving and nearly hit someone, you remind yourself to be more cautious and you take control.

Why is it that when you're overthinking and feeling anxious, that you continue running marathons in your mind with your thoughts? As you look at the things in your life that you change so freely, ask yourself why you can't do the same with the narrative of your thoughts.

It's time to change the channel in your mind.

Turn it down.

Turn it off.

MIND
MAPPING

At 18 years old, young Michael very simply gifted his friend a penknife. Later that evening he fell deep into thought where he began to worry what his friend may do with the knife, where he worryingly considered every worst-case scenario possible. As he went from thought to thought, he felt crippling anxiety and fear as his fingertips were on the penknife he had gifted. His worry turned to ideas, thoughts and mental constructions of him ending up in trouble with the police should the knife be used in any negative way that could come back to his fingerprints being on the knife. Even though his friend did nothing with the knife and nothing serious was to ever come from the gift that was given, Michael couldn't shift the feelings of anxiety and often considered the possible negative consequences, which never actually came true. This filled him with anxiety and the more he thought about it, the more fear he felt.

Months later, he found himself beginning to analyse how he had communicated to a fellow student in general conversation. Nothing negative, insulting or serious was said to cause any concern; however, he began to overthink and over-analyse what he had said and if it could have been taken in a negative way that could lead to him possibly getting into trouble. Nothing ever happened from the general conversation, although the pattern began to continue weeks later where Michael again started to over-analyse his spoken words from an entirely different situation. As he kept thinking back to what he had said, and whether the words he had spoken could in any way lead him to be in trouble should they be "taken in the wrong direction", he was overpowered with anxiety. He was now 22 years old as he sat opposite me in his coaching session. The pattern had run weekly for four years where he described in his own words how he had become a shell of his former self. Riddled with the feelings of anxiety where he would often overthink and then over-feel, as his mind and his thoughts had fallen into disempowering habitual patterns of anxiety, he felt powerless.

Anxious thoughts will always lead to anxious feelings. The feelings that are created from the thoughts that you think are like a pathway that you walk down in your mind. Each step and each visit can make the route in your mind easier to access where you frequently walk the path of anxiety, thinking and feeling your way through anxious thoughts. If your thoughts for what you see in your mind and what you say to yourself with your inner voice are in some ways "newer" then the journey down the pathway of anxiety will feel as though you are on a new path. If however, you have repeated the thoughts over any period of time, the new path will have turned into a more frequent path that your brain is used to accessing, even without thinking, and you may find yourself deeper down this all-too-familiar path than you desired. Any new route that you physically walk in your life can take time to get used to. Any familiar route that you take, you will probably walk or drive down without paying any attention to your all-so-familiar surroundings. This is and was the same for Michael and may well be the case for you, where you are finding yourself quite far down the path of anxiety, which feels familiar, uncomfortable and an effort to walk away from. The key is to form better pathways in your mind with your thinking, which lead to better routes that are more comfortable to walk in through your mind and your body. Any new route is formed through the thoughts that you think, and for most people changing the direction of their thinking can seem like a huge effort to turn the direction in their mind. **If you want to feel peace, you must think peaceful thoughts.** If you want to experience a sense of calm, you must journey down and even create the pathways of calm so that they exist in your mind. Once you have established any pathway that you wish to take, it will become easier for you to access, feel, experience and journey down through the thoughts that you think yourself through. When you know what is familiar, it becomes habitual and easy to go with what you know, and this is often the way with anxiety. Your mind can habitually take you on that journey that you don't want to go on with your thoughts, but if that's all your mind knows then that's where your mind will take you. A big part of the antidote is to change and interrupt the pattern of your current anxious thinking. You will have previously taken my guidance to recall different past memories which would have led you to feel the feelings associated with those memories. This may have felt easy to think and access or quite the effort to then think and feel. The key is to repeat the steps with what you're thinking so that those steeping stones that you're experiencing through your thoughts can quickly turn into a pathway that is easy to walk in your mind. Whether it makes sense for you to change the channel of your thoughts, or the station that you're listening to with your thinking, or the pathway your mind is walking along, any change is going to become easier with practice and repetition. You can **pattern interrupt** your thoughts and use **pause** to stop your visual thoughts and **turn the volume down** to silence your internal dialogue. It can also be helpful to then actively shift your mindset from feeling powerless to being powerful.

You may not have realized it, but you may have become an expert at thinking through all the possible worst-case scenarios. This future planning may have left you feeling like you were gaining a sense of control, but it has probably exhausted you with anxiety. To break this pathway of thinking and to train your mind to make new and more positive journeys with your thoughts, this next method encourages you to walk in a new direction in your mind. Instead of thinking about every worse-case scenario, how about spending time thinking through the best possible outcomes?

EXERCISE: THE BEST-CASE SCENARIO METHOD

VISUAL THINKER OPTION

1. Identify how you are thinking. Are you watching scene after scene in your mind of thoughts that are leading you to feel anxious? Actively change the images and scenes inside your head by thinking up 5–10 positive scenarios and situations that are not negative and anxiety-inducing.

For example, if you are thinking that you are going to act or look stupid in a social situation, which leaves you feeling anxious and uneasy about being social, change the narrative or thoughts for the better, by changing the direction of the mental pathway you are journeying down in the map of your internal thoughts.

- Think of, visualize and produce the internal representation of you being social with ease, confidence and with a sense of enjoyment.
- If you can think back to a specific time where you felt a sense of social ease and enjoyment, revisit this mental scenario first and make it as vivid and real as possible in your mind. Then take the feelings and imagine yourself again having a social time of enjoyment and ease in the future, to help train and re-focus your train of thought.

- If you cannot recall one, construct a set of images and thoughts that help you to feel calmer within yourself. Give yourself time and practice and allow yourself to move forward feeling more in control and at ease from the thoughts that you are choosing to focus your time and energy on inside your mind.
- Think of anywhere between 5–10 scenarios in your mind for the area that you're thinking and feeling anxious for by changing the thoughts so that they are more positive.

AUDITORY THINKER OPTION

2. Identify how you are thinking. Are you listening to inner voices in your mind of thoughts that are leading you to feel anxious? Actively change the voices inside your head by thinking up 5–10 positive scenarios and situations that are not negative and anxiety-inducing.

- Have a positive inner conversation and use words and phrases that lead you to override the anxiety that you feel. If you can spend time hearing yourself saying the fearful words and conversations that induce the feelings of anxiety in your body, change the direction of your internal communication away from what you fear.
- What could you say to yourself to make yourself think and feel better?
- What is it that you need to hear?
- Instead of spending time thinking about the possible threats of uncertainty, affirm what you do know. Tell

yourself words or phrases of reassurance. Hear yourself feeling safe and in control from what you are saying. Write out a list of calm affirmations or sentences of reassurance that you can use and hear with your inner voice. Examples: "I am calm", "I am safe", "I can relax and focus on the present moment", "I am in control of my thoughts". Making a personal list and connecting with the feelings that the words you hear make you feel can and will help improve your emotional state and quickly.

- Spend time actively utilizing the power to communicate freely and more consciously inside of yourself by actively channelling your inner voice to positively serve you and empower how you feel.

In taking ownership of the actions of your mind with regards to your thoughts, to then help improve the way that you feel within yourself, the key is in you changing the channel of your mind for the better. This exercise should help you create new pathways and thought patterns to transform the inner map of your mind.

How does it feel to consider and think through thoughts that lead you to feel reassured, certain, at ease and in control?

I encourage you to practise both the visual option and the auditory option for 30 days. Aim to be consistent and interrupt the anxious thought patterns as they occur, and then shift to being more present with your **Personal GPS**.

The mental movies that you create within, along with the inner sounds produced from your inner voices, do not have to run riot, destroying your sense of inner peace. Giving yourself time to consider your options but instead now more positively, as you choose to think and communicate them within, can once again reduce the impact of anxiety as you actively shift your focus from the potential bad to all of the potential and possible good that you can think of. I suggest that you start to use the **mind mapping method** as and when needed for 30 days. Aim to be consistent and interrupt the anxious thought patterns to shift from fear-based thinking to more positive thoughts through various times of your day, and then shift to being more present with your **Personal GPS**. 30 days of straight practice of **mind mapping** can help you develop a more habitual skill of using the pattern interrupt to shift from anxiety to inner peace and it can weaken the anxious thoughts the more that you use it.

YOUR PERSONAL GPS:
SHIFT AND BECOME

Awareness and action lead to a new map of the world. As you soak in all that's new and learn how to navigate more empowering ways of being, look past these words and, for a few minutes, see, hear and feel the space around you.

TAMING
THE BEAST

"You're not good enough", "You won't get this job", "If you get sick no one will save you", "They think you're stupid", "It will go wrong", "You're going to die"...

Have you ever really listened to the words that your inner voice is saying? Most people wouldn't allow another person to say what their inner voice says to them inside their head, and yet most people who have a difficult inner voice have no idea how to stop it from causing them to feel mental and emotional distress.

I often tell my students who are training on my NLP practitioner courses the story of the time I discovered my anxious inner voice. It was years after one of the anxiety experiences I had endured before a music video audition. My career before moving into personal wellness and coaching was in the music and television industry, where I worked with recording artists and brands as a professional dancer. I had danced from the age of 13, enrolled in professional training aged 18 and began working professionally while still training in my professional training. My confidence levels were through the roof. As I look back at the younger version of myself who was so passionate about dancing, who was full of hope with endless dreams of the types of performing jobs that I wanted to do, back then I believed that I was going to get booked on a job before the audition had even started. There wasn't an ounce of doubt in my mind. I was confident and I'd like to say humble, and it was during my training in NLP that I began to look back on the mindset I had in those younger years and identify a significant audition experience as the point at which my confidence had started to change and where, unknown to me then, I was in fact experiencing anxiety.

There was a pattern of behaviour that had started to develop in some larger auditions. Where the room was full of hundreds of dancers waiting to audition for eight employable positions, like an out-of-body experience, I found myself removing myself from the room and not going through with the audition. I was years into my career, I had ticked off many of the jobs I had dreamed of doing, but something had changed within me where I began to question my abilities, which pulled down my confidence. I found myself listening to a voice inside my head that was causing me to feel very uncomfortable in my own body. The voice of anxiety had surfaced and without my awareness quickly grown in its communication, which would often tell me: "I wasn't good enough", "I wasn't going to get this job" and that "I should leave to save myself from the embarrassment and rejection I would feel." I was unaware of this voice being anxiety at the time. As I look back, I remember how the voice and what it would communicate inside my head would leave me feeling on edge, physically sick and at times an overwhelming sense of panic. In one particular audition where I waited with friends and colleagues to start the audition process for a music video that Madonna was filming in London, the voice of anxiety was so overwhelming that I felt the room was closing in on me and my only way out was to leave.

Back then, I wasn't aware of any of my inner voices, and I certainly had no idea of how I could work with the voice of anxiety that was causing me to feel so uncomfortable in my own skin. As a master practitioner and trainer of NLP, I have worked with hundreds of people across the world who all have a voice of anxiety inside their head that forms a part of their anxiety experience, showing them how to have more control over the voice that taunts them within, so that they can relieve the feelings of anxiety. The results are often described as "heavenly", when a person suddenly hears only silence within the walls of their mind.

In developing your awareness for how your inner voice is communicating, by listening more when it talks to you, really hearing what it says and, most importantly, by working with your inner critic, you can put an end to its reign of terror. If left to its own accord, the voices will continue to tease, taunt and torment you. The strength and determination to pull your focus down a pathway of negative thinking and feeling will overpower you if you do not silence your inner critic and develop a more empowering and mindful way of thinking and communicating for yourself. This installation of a voice that allows you to think and feel better should then be exercised daily to develop strength, open communication and control for how you talk to yourself through your thoughts, to better improve your mental and emotional health.

Whether it's a voice that talks at you that is expressing anxiety, or an inner conversation that you may find yourself taking part in or witnessing as an observer, the thoughts you have can be a big factor of your mental and emotional anxiety.

Quite often the underlying feeling that is fuelling the voice to speak in an overpowering, frantic and anxious way is the need for **safety**. When you potentially feel unsafe, out of control, uncertain, worried and even fearful, the need for safety within can feel compromised, which can cause your inner voice to turn on the voice of anxiety.

Telling you *"You're not good enough"* may be your mind's way of preventing you from doing things that could lead to feeling embarrassed in front of other people. *"You're going to die"* could be a fear response to you driving on the motorway, where your mind chooses this way of trying to get your attention to keep you safe, instead of telling you to be cautious and slow when you drive.

The safety aspect of your inner voice could be feeling into past experiences, whether recent or further back to your younger years. You may have had a bad experience with public speaking in your youth, for example, and your inner voice is using words like "You're going to stutter and freeze up on stage" in order to prevent you going through the same experience again.

EXERCISE: TAMING THE ANXIOUS INNER VOICE METHOD

1. Tune in to your anxious inner voice and listen closely.
2. What is the voice saying?
3. How loud is the voice on a scale of 1 to 10 (10 being the loudest)?
4. What speed is it talking at?
5. What is the tone of the voice?
6. How old is the voice?
7. Consider if what the voice is saying is in any way trying to keep you safe.
8. Hear what the voice has to say specifically through your thoughts in relation to the area of anxiety in your life.
9. Feel, sense, consider or even ask if the voice is communicating in relation to a specific past experience more so than the current situation it feels anxious about.
10. You can use your remote control method and start now, turn the volume down to zero to turn the voice of anxiety off.

Once you have explored the voice in some detail, you can then take your findings and start to address what it is your anxiety wants and needs in the next method which can help address further the voice or any thoughts of anxiety.

YOUR PERSONAL GPS

From breathing to changing the channel of your mind to a space and place of inner peace, take a moment to direct your awareness to being freely in the present moment. Look past these words and, for a few minutes, **see**, **hear** and **feel** the space around you.

UNDERSTANDING YOUR ANXIOUS WANTS AND NEEDS

From an NLP point of view, I often look for the "wants" and "needs" that are driving the anxiety that the person is experiencing. It is quite common to have an underlying "driver" that is pushing and quite literally driving the behaviour and possible emotions for any area of your life. You can have a motivation "driver" and a different "driver" for your health and even career, where within yourself there lies beliefs, values and experiences that formulate the "drive" that leads you to feel and experience your particular emotions. Most people are unconsciously aware of what it is their anxiety wants or what it needs, as it really can be a messenger calling from within as the particular "want" or "need" of the anxiety is the driver. You can turn your inner voice down all day long, but you can go further in your understanding and your interventions by getting to know the feelings behind the wants and needs that are behind the anxious thoughts that are leaving you feeling on edge.

When working with clients, if you do not identify and even address the potential wants and needs behind their anxiety that is driving their experience, the anxiety may in effect begin to communicate in other ways. You may find your anxiety expressing itself through further thought patterns or communications. You may even find yourself suddenly experiencing unhealthy behaviour that causes you to feel and be distracted from the feelings of anxiety. Overly drinking alcohol, smoking and drug use are a few extreme examples of ways that people find themselves finding short-term relief, which over time can become an increased and uncomfortable new problem in their life.

The key is to consider, what is driving this behaviour? What does my anxiety want or need from me to feel better?

The next part of the process of working with your mindset as an extended part of understanding your anxiety and taming your inner voice, is to question and communicate with the words and conversations or the visual pictures and scenes that are being had within your thoughts. It's fine to talk to yourself. Remember, most people are having internal talks and are not really listening to what is being said. If you were to say some of the things that you were hearing inside your own head with your inner voice out aloud, how would you feel? Would you even say some of the things that you say to yourself out aloud to someone else?

Let's consider discovering more from your anxiety and your anxious inner voice by formulating a communication to potentially better understand what it is that you are experiencing and potentially why.

EXERCISE: WANTS AND NEEDS EXPLORATION METHOD

1. Ask your anxiety, "What is it that you **want**?" Allow yourself time to pause so that an understanding can arise.

2. Ask your anxiety, "What is it that you **need**?" Grant yourself a pause to allow an answer to come.

3. Once you have come to an understanding of what is driving your anxiety, tell your inner voice what it needs to hear, either aloud or in your mind. Imagine talking to a young child that is in need of reassurance. What specifically would you say to the child to help the child feel better? Consider then, what you may say to your anxiety? Aim to be rational, specific and direct.

4. If the anxiety continues to communicate, talk back to it, offering guidance and reassurance.

5. Get to a point where you can close the conversation down with authority, having the final word of reassurance and advice that you then consciously accept and move forward with.

6. Once you have addressed the wants and needs with your inner voice and closed the internal conversation, practise once again being present. See, hear and feel, and mute or turn down the volume or pause and move any visual thoughts as you then observe the silent space and place of your mind.

A lady I worked with told me her inner voice constantly told her she "wasn't good enough" for a job she was thinking of applying for. After using the following method, however, she realized that the anxiety only wanted to keep her **safe** from what it perceived to be a vulnerable position in the interview. It "needed" comfort, so the voice of anxiety told her not to bother, so that she could remain in her comfort zone and not be put on the spot.

A daily practice of using any of the mentioned methods to help you work on your visual- and auditory-based thoughts can help you to break the habitual patterns of anxious thinking. In interrupting the patterns of thinking by changing the channel, ending the cycle and in using your visual thoughts as well as your inner voices in more positive, reassuring and calming ways, you can again retrain the way that your mind is operating to transform how you feel within.

In breaking the patterns, you can also then practise shifting to the present moment by being more mindful with your **Personal GPS**. The self-exploration to address the **wants** and **needs** that drive your experience can also help you to change the communication from panic to reassurance where needed within your thinking.

ANSWER THE PHONE

The call from within gets stronger and more persistent the longer you ignore its wants and needs. Who is the caller known as "Anxiety"? Answer the phone. Listen and observe the anxious thoughts for what your anxiety wants and what your anxiety needs. There's possibilities of peace from accepting the call. Turn your focus within.

DEACTIVATE
YOUR ANXIETY

Earlier in the book we spoke about the heightened awareness that can be caused by anxiety, and how it is triggered by your nervous system. This section will show you how to switch this feeling of alarm off.

One of the many ways that can help you to ground and centre, feel calm and collected, is through breathing.

When you are anxious, your sympathetic nervous system will be active, regulating your body into "flight or fight" mode. In this heightened awareness, your brain resembles a home alarm sensor, naturally scanning and searching the parameters of your life for any potential threats. Your body responds by switching to shallow breathing, which is its way of preparing you for the "threat" (real or perceived) that you are about to face.

Changing the flow and pattern of your breathing can do wonders for how you feel inside, and it can also have an immediate and rewarding effect on your physical body. You can consider this as the code to disarm your internal anxiety alarm. The powerful shift that you can experience through your breathing can also be paired with the practice of being mindful, which can also aid you in achieving immediate relief from the way that your mind and body feels.

I often encounter anxious smokers both personally and professionally. Without the use of a vape or cigarette, the individual usually presents a very short shallow breath that they are living with. Tight restricted lungs, where the capacity of the breath remains surface level and shallow will not allow you to feel calm. Smokers tend to inhale the cigarette or vape deeply. Hence the reason behind the continual action of smoking, where each person is consciously and actively breathing. The difficulty with smoking is that there is a third part involved between the airway opening and the breath to be taken. This is usually the cigarette or vape. I always encourage clients to replace the device with a straw and to inhale deeply as though they are taking a usual "drag" to then exhale, moving the straw away. Most of the times it fulfils the same action and need. The individual has removed themselves to an outdoor area to smoke, to take a break from their routine, and now encouraged to inhale through a straw, the person now takes in a large, deep inhale of air. Exhaling allows them to calm down, and when timing two minutes of breathing, the individual then feels more at ease. The key is to open up and expand the lungs. The more air that goes in, the more reward you can and will feel from the natural and consciously directed action and direction of breathing. You cannot fully feel anxious when you feel relaxed. If you experience a shortness and sharpness of breath, the chances are that you will be feeling physically, mentally and emotionally on edge.

The aim of this part of the Anxiety Antidote is to allow you to breathe, to take action to disengage the overactive side of your nervous system that is leading you to be in an anxious sate. Breathing is inexpensive. Conscious breathing can help change your focus and the direction of your thoughts. Breathing is rewarding and easy to do anywhere and at any time. Allow yourself to feel the powerful shift that breathing can have on your anxiety. The key is to be patient and persistent. Most people, especially those who shallow breathe, find it difficult to open up their airways to let their breath in. It's like doing a physical stretch. Tight hamstrings can take time to feel loose, although expanding and increasing your lung capacity can be achieved quicker than you think. During those first few breaths, even if they feel short and shallow, keep persevering. You may yawn, but this is a sign that your body is opening up to more air and oxygen. You may also feel lightheaded, and this is the body's way of telling you that more air is getting in. Be seated when you are practising your breathing and encourage yourself to breathe slowly and deeply.

As you develop a breathing practice where you can also **turn down** any inner sounds, **pause** any thoughts and practise using your senses to **be present** in your time and space, you can give yourself a daily breathing practice to fully receive the benefits of active conscious breathing. The first option is about breathing and also directing your focus and working a little on your thoughts.

EXERCISE:
THE ALARM CODE METHOD

OPTION 1: FOLLOW THE BREATH

1. Sitting comfortably, take a slow, long, deep breath, inhaling and exhaling fully to allow your lungs to expand and open. Do this 15 times.

2. With each inhale and exhale, mindfully count each breath to stay focused, and encourage each inhale to be longer and deeper, exhaling fully between each breath.

3. Focus your awareness and your attention on each breath. Follow the breath in, keep your focus and attention on the inhale, and follow the breath out.

4. As you shift your mind from any thoughts to the flow and rhythm of each of the 15 breaths, you will develop your ability to shift your focus at any time that you need to, away from any anxious thoughts.

Top tip: Encourage your inhale to be soft as you inhale through the nose, and exhale fully through the mouth, as if you are gently blowing out a candle. Direct each breath deep into your lungs by aiming to breathe into your stomach. Allow your belly to expand and rise on the inhale and to gently fall and recede back in with each exhale.

OPTION 2: GIVING YOURSELF TIME TO BREATHE

This next option can help you to prolong the experience of conscious breathing and to also practise combining your additional antidote methods.

1. Set a timer on your phone or device for 10 minutes. Find a space where you are undisturbed and allow yourself to sit, focus and breathe. Notice how each inhale becomes longer and deeper, and how with each exhale you can feel calmer and more relaxed within your mind and body.

Option 1 allows you to follow the breath and feel a shift through 15 slow conscious breaths.

Option 2 allows you to have an undisturbed time of 10 minutes to sit and reap the benefits of breathing.

Giving yourself time to breathe will allow you to feel relaxed mentally, emotionally and especially physically. Consciously breathing can allow you time to be mindful, to focus on your breath and to interrupt the patterns of thoughts that may be causing your anxiety. Encourage yourself to spend some time each day for the next 30 days where you have time to actively breathe and practise these breathing exercises to feel the shift mentally and emotionally within.

As well as breathing exercises, other activities that help your nervous system feel more balanced include:

- Yoga
- Meditation
- Practising mindfulness
- Viewing or creating art
- Slow walking
- Spending time in nature
- Listening to relaxing music
- Sound baths
- Having a massage
- Chi kung (qi gong)
- Tai chi
- Chanting
- Expressing gratitude

DECLUTTER

With each inhale you are opening the doorways of peace and allowing any elements of anxiety to vacate your body as you exhale. There's so much power for the mind and body in a simple yet powerful set of breaths.

THE CONTROL ROOM
OF YOUR MIND

It's quite common to have a variety of feelings that produce a sense of discomfort that travels through your body when you are having an anxiety experience. From unpleasant feelings in your gut to heaviness anchoring your body into feeling lethargic. Even trembling can at times take over your body. Increased panic breathing that leads to the sensation that you can't take in any more air and that you may hyperventilate, as well as a fast heart rate, can also leave you feeling very uncomfortable in the body that you live in. On the surface it may look as though nothing much is happening; however, on the inside the unpleasant experience can leave you looking like you've entered into a state of shock. As you now begin to work from the centre point of the control room of your mind to improve how you think, how you breathe, how present you can be and how you work with your inner voices, you can also use the following method to help you feel more at ease in your own skin.

On a work trip to Mauritius, where I was travelling to teach a week's wellness programme in the sun, I suddenly found myself in a bout of anxiety that was sprung on to me from the turbulence of the flight. Out of nowhere the plane began moving, the seatbelt sign was switched and sounded on, and the anxiety that I experienced in my mind, which operated at a great speed, led me to believe this could be the end of my life. My awareness kicked in that I needed to take control. It was the feelings that were running through my body that signalled most the discomfort that fed the panicked voice inside my head to produce the anxiety within. The feelings were **located in my gut** and were **moving upward** like an elevator at quite a **speed**, which left me feeling as though I was going to be sick. The feelings that **moved like a cylinder**, that were quite **thick in shape** and **strong** in their strength tore through my core centre continually **moving upward**. As I felt the feelings and noticed that both of my hands were gripping on to the arm rests of the seat with great strength, I knew that I had to act immediately on this sudden surprise of physical anxiety. I realized that I needed to work firstly on the feelings and by taking the position of my awareness and directions of my thoughts, I mentally took hold of the feelings and "made" them move downwards instead of upwards. Reversing the feeling and at the same time relaxing my arms, releasing the seat grip, I continued to mentally "make" the movements move down towards my navel and then continued to move them down each leg, holding them into the soles of my feet. Feeling the weight drop to my feet, my arms continued to relax and I swiftly "**muted**" the voice in my head that was screaming, "You are going to die." I took several deep calming breaths, as I saw, heard and also felt my feet on the floor, to feel more anchored and at ease in my seat. A minute later the turbulence had stopped, and a final deep breath in, leading me to relax further into my seat, allowed me to continue with my in-flight movie as both the anxiety and turbulence had disappeared. You have to actively put the brakes on your anxious feelings, and you must choose to take control over your thoughts. This next area to look at can help you to improve the kinaesthetic aspects of your anxiety, **the feelings** that you experience within your body.

From personal and professional experience, uncomfortable feelings in the body usually recede when you work on the thoughts that you see and watch inside your mind and the sounds that you say and hear to yourself. As you intervene on a thought pattern or sound you may find immediate relief in your mind, and in most cases a reduction, if not a cancellation of the feelings that are then felt and experienced within your body. The following methods allow you to "make" more of the outcome that you desire.

EXERCISE: MAKE YOUR MIND DIRECT YOUR BODY METHOD

1. Mentally pinpoint the location of the sensations you feel within your body when you are anxious. Churning in your gut? Trembling hands? Legs feeling like jelly?
2. Notice the movement of these sensations. Identify if there is a pattern of the movement – forward and back, round and round, or perhaps pulsing?
3. Notice a speed. Is it fast or slow? Constant or intermittent?
4. Now direct your mind to the area where you feel the feelings and make the feeling change. For example, "make it pause", "make it still", "make it reverse", "make it weak", "make it softer". Whether you consider a remote-control action, or control room that you enter, your mind can and will direct your body to do what is required.

You do not have to feel uncomfortable inside your own body. In using the above method to locate the feelings, to work with them to create a sense of ease within yourself, you can begin to use your mind to take control of over the feelings of anxiety that your body experiences.

SUNRISE

Step into the peace with purpose. Breathe in each new day which is available with each and every moment. You have stopped the journey that feels out of control. You have made the choice to be free and the steps are there waiting patiently for you to climb up to higher levels of inner harmony. The clouds are clear, and the light will open your eyes to experience the way that is more freeing on the outside that clears you out of stuck ways that have been felt and experienced time after time within. Be open. Live in the light of your mind, for the lower levels are nothing compared to the freedom that you can so easily experience for your own mind, body and soul. Smile.

TRIGGERED

A single sight of something that you see, or a particular sound can transport you back to a past experience that causes you to re-live past anxious feelings and emotions. You may see or hear something and then find yourself mentally back re-playing difficult episodes of the past that disturb your present peace. This can feel overwhelming and in other cases you can see or hear something that then causes you to think ahead to future possible anxious situations, again removing you from the present moment. Being triggered can happen by taking you back, or with anxiety it can mentally and emotionally propel you forward into the concerns of the unknown. You may use your senses to assess potential threats in certain places and situations, but a lot of moments that can trigger a person can happen unconsciously.

If there have been past significant emotional experiences of anxiety, you may end up triggered in the present moment from something that you see or hear, which causes you to mentally and emotionally connect back to parts of those past difficult experiences. Going back to the NLP communication model for how you take in each moment of each experience, which is then filtered through your senses, you may see, hear or smell something that then presently triggers you. This external stimulus may then mentally take you back to replay a past episode that can be the cause of your present anxiety. This can also happen where you have a set of thoughts that come to mind and again from what you see or hear, you may be triggered to feel anxiety but this time from the internal representations of your thoughts that instead cause you to think ahead with anxiety. Some of your triggers may be external that your senses consciously and unconsciously sense, and others can be thought patterns that you experience within that then trigger your anxiety. This in some ways can happen without you knowing that a visual aspect or a sound in your present space can trigger you. If you find that you are having flashbacks to past difficult memories, you may be experiencing post-traumatic stress disorder. I highly recommend that you have Integral Eye Movement Therapy (IEMT) sessions, which can rapidly help deal with flashbacks, past traumas and anxiety triggers.

Following an incident as a teenager where I had been approached and mugged walking in broad daylight, I had various flashbacks of the event that would replay very quickly through my mind. I would see the visual thoughts and feel the feelings as the thoughts would pop up on the screen of my mind. This caused me to feel mentally and emotionally low as I re-lived the situation time and time again through my thoughts. For years, what proceeded the event was that, in public spaces in particular large crowds, around loud noises and even when walking or travelling in certain areas, I found myself triggered by my surroundings, overly feeling anxious from the idea of another possible negative experience. Without realizing, I would be overly sensitive wherever I was, looking around (visually scanning), listening (using my auditory sense) for the search of any possible potential threats. This constantly left me on edge and in fight or flight mode as I consciously and a lot of the time unconsciously felt I needed to be on alert and ready to flee for safety.

For one lady that I worked with, she could be going about her day-to-day life where she would be triggered to feel overwhelming anxiety from the sound of a phone ring. This took her back to a past difficult phone call where she had received some bad news. This left her on edge and years after the experience had passed, she still felt triggered by the sound of the phone. The significant emotional experience had led her to then remain in fight or flight mode for long periods of each day. Most sounds left her feeling anxious. She would regularly look at and check her phone and the actual ring and sound of a message would also trigger her into a state of overwhelming panic. Her triggers would cause her to think ahead for the worst and for the present moment. Her significant emotional experience didn't cause her to flashback, but to flash forward with an inner voice and visuals of panic and anxiety.

Some people can experience flashbacks that are visually vivid in their mind which floods their body with uncomfortable feelings in the present moment. There are also triggers that can cause a person anxiety but not have any past flashbacks. A trigger can action a mental thought pattern of anxiety to suddenly walk the mental pathway of anxious thinking. Just as I would think ahead for possible worst-case situations as a teenager, from one difficult significant emotional experience, a single sight or sound of a possible threat can trigger the mind to play out anxious thoughts. If the person has then regularly thought about possible future threats that leaves them feelings anxious, then the trigger can cause them to activate and then get caught up with the cycle of overthinking that leaves them feeling anxious. This can feel overwhelming because usually the person has walked this mental pathway time and time again and suddenly from the trigger, they find themselves so far in their mind ahead in the worst-case scenarios deep in their anxious thoughts. If you find you are triggered to overthink future-based situations that leave you feeling anxious, you must interrupt the thought patterns to break the cycle of thinking. Breaking the thought patterns can help you weaken the connection of thoughts and distance yourself from the pathway that you get lost in within your thinking. It may also help to use the journaling process to write out times where you are safe, not anxious, and times where you thought about possible threats but then they never happened. This can again help you to remove and expand the deletion filter of your thinking that may be only scanning for possible threats. Should you find yourself thinking back to past difficult memories, the following NLP process can help you to work on those thoughts and any flashbacks.

From personal experience where I've had different levels of PTSD three times in my life, from having various flashbacks and difficulties feeling anything but anxiety, living on high alert can be debilitating. I strongly recommend that you consider any form of anxiety, but in particular flashbacks, as a call to action from within. If you frequently feel on edge, in a state of panic, and if you have flashbacks to past difficult experiences, you must answer the call from within that is asking for your help and assistance. This call to action is in many ways communicating to you that resolutions are needed for you to return to your normal "factory settings" that do not require you to be on high alert. For many people the difficult experiences and challenges can live on for years in the mind and be felt in the body for long periods of time that do not have to happen. The continual triggered episodes that pull a person back or propel a person to being on high alert thinking ahead can have a long-term negative impact on your health and nervous system. Personalities and behaviours can change, relationships can become effected, and dreams and goals can get lost in the trauma of anxiety. Answering the call from within can help bring peace, harmony and a reset to the mind and body that can be achieved with professional help. Consider slowly working through the following methods and if further intervention is required, please seek out an experienced IEMT master practitioner.

There are three parts to this next method. The first helps you to comfortably establish some safe and resourceful shifting state methods should you find the areas you are working on too emotionally overwhelming. Please spend some time first working through part 1 to get into a safe space. Part 2 helps you work on the difficult past memories and part 3 will help you to actively use your mind in a more powerful way to help you shift how you think and feel for the better.

EXERCISE: FLASHBACKS/ NEGATIVE MEMORIES METHOD

PART 1

1. In a safe and sensible place, where you feel undisturbed to focus on working through your thoughts and experiences, it is important to first establish some positive resources that you can access should you need them.

2. Think of (you may already have them from past suggestions) specific memories from your past where you felt: 1. Safe. 2. Calm. 3. Relaxed.

3. List two examples for each state and label each memory: for example, Safe – 1. At home on the sofa. 2. In the presence of a friend or partner. Calm – 1. Sitting in the garden. 2. During meditation. Relaxed – 1. In the bath. 2. Lying in bed. Get clear on your examples and have them as a list.

4. When you have your examples spend three minutes thinking about each example as if you are there in the safe, calm, relaxed space. See what you see in your mind. Hear the space and place of each memory and most importantly feel the safe, calm and relaxed feelings in your body.

5. Repeat this process of recalling and revisiting these past experiences three times so that they are vivid and easy to recall in your mind. It is important to set up these

safe, calm and relaxed responses that you can access and shift from any overwhelming negative feelings should you need.

PART 2

1. Write down each flashback to work on. It could be one single word that identifies the flashback, so you don't need to go into great detail about the experience.
2. Work on one memory at a time and, if needed, have a break between each one before working on the next if there are a few that you want to work on.

Now read through the next parts first from start to finish before you apply the steps.

1. Close your eyes and bring to mind the flashback memory.
2. Press PAUSE on the mental movie you see so that the image of the person or situation is still.
3. Make the image you see blurry and unfocused. Notice the shift in how it feels.
4. Now make the blurry image very dark so that it is harder to see.
5. Shrink it down and make it smaller and smaller and smaller.
6. Mentally move the small, dark image far off into the distance behind you. Make it disappear.
7. Lock this in place behind you so that you can't see it or feel it, with all of these changes.

8. Open your eyes. See, hear and feel your space around you. Become present.

9. Think about the old memory and notice how it has changed for you.

10. Repeat the whole process for any other flashbacks, or difficult memories. Work on one memory at a time and, if needed, have a break before moving on to the next flashback.

11. Break state, see, hear, feel. Try some breathing exercises and calmly move on with your day.

Further work moving forward.

USING YOUR INNER VOICE

1. Action your inner voice. Begin by saying to yourself, "I am free of the past."

2. Follow this by saying, "I deal with one day at a time."

3. Now actively continue to use your inner voice to increase and produce a sense of feeling calm, reassured and in control.

4. Write a list of five things for each emotional state: calm, reassured and to feel in control.

5. Read out each phrase internally with your inner voice and connect to the feelings that the words that you hear are creating within.

6. Turn the volume up to a comfortable level that you can hear inside your head to feel the shifts.

7. Actively use your inner voice on a daily basis and any time you may feel triggered to think back or ahead so that you can shift from anxiety to a sense of calm, to feeling reassured and in control.

You can also engage in some journaling to again help you move forward with your mindset and your thoughts. It can be common practice to focus on the aspects of your reality that leave you feeling anxious. To move past this way of thinking and to open your mind to avoid deleting any aspect of safety, certainty or self-control that may be part of your actual reality, simply write a list now of 10 things today or from this week that were not anxiety experiences, or focus your attention on how you are feeling better each day with evidence that supports these positive feelings in the lists that you write.

Following this process, should you feel any uncomfortable feelings in your body, sit and breathe slowly and deeply for 10 minutes and practise your **Personal GPS** to see, hear and feel to ground into your personal space.

YOUR PERSONAL GPS –

FLOWING INSIDE OUT

As the world within your mental and emotional body feels lighter the freedom of the present space is always there. Take a moment to practise, to shift, to feel and direct your awareness to being freely in the present moment. Look past these words and for a few minutes, see, hear and feel the space and place around. Be present. See, hear and feel.

EXPIRY DATE

Inspiration comes to every individual. Anxious thoughts have a shelf life, whereas inspiration is endless. As you look outside of yourself, be inspired. As you walk forward, feel inspired. Let your time and energy light up the pathways of your mind, formulating connections which flow like a natural waterfall into every cell of your being. As you feel the clarity cascading down from your mind, imagine each thought is a drip of inspiration that forms a rainbow of light that lifts you out of being stuck. Put your wings on and fly, by flying through your thoughts.

BECOMING ACCOUNTABLE

What might becoming accountable and creating a personalized Anxiety Antidote look like for different people and cases of anxiety? Let's take a look.

Anna devised a list of five phrases that she could use to think in more resourceful ways and move her away from any anxious thinking. Specifically, Anna needed to feel in control, calm and not anxious when she was driving. She often found that with two young children in the back of the car she needed to feel safe on the road, which now often required her talking to, or in some safe ways checking on, her children. Her five phrases were used before and during her driving as she would often **turn down** the voice of anxiety and **activate her inner voice of reassurance** in a more resourceful way. Interrupting the current pattern and then actively using her inner voice to offer herself some reassuring words helped her to feel more confident to then drive. Her active shift in her thinking for the way in which her mind was working allowed her to take control and not be controlled by her anxiety.

Ajay felt out of place at school, in particular socially with his fellow peers. He had withdrawn over time and stayed out of any large group action. He wanted this to change so that he could enjoy his time with his friends but his fears and overthinking often led him to feel anxious and withdrawn. He began to stop the patterns of overthinking that he would play out in his mind. He had spent too much time walking down the pathways of "what if" with his thoughts that had only made the feelings of anxiety stronger and more uncomfortable to deal with. He had thought through endless possible and potential embarrassing situations that could happen in front of his fellow school peers, which left him feeling anxious. He had let his mind create so much fear and let the negative feelings win that he felt his only choice was to withdraw. He first began to **make regular daily lists** for the number of times he actually didn't embarrass himself, where school life was easy, fun and enjoyable and he was not at all anxious. The lists started to loosen his grip on the problem in his mind and his fixation on his anxiety as he began to expand his deletion filter by actively noticing and recording the times he wasn't anxious. He then **switched his thinking to visualize positive possible outcomes.** Having learned how he could change the way he was thinking from what could go wrong **to what could go right**, he immediately felt calmer and looked forward to school. This again was a daily practice where he interrupted the anxious thought patterns. He would **actively interrupt the pattern of habitual anxious thinking** that was causing him to feel anxious, and instead create scenes, scenarios and lists that left him feeling in control. The new patterns began to get stronger, easier to think of and allowed him to become more engaged and involved with his school life.

Olivia would out of nowhere feel anxious in her gut, which led her body to sweat and her mind to feel confused, as she could see no obvious reason to feel anxious. There were times where she would wake in the morning feeling on edge, and other times where she began to worry that the gut churning and physical sweats would come on in public. Having introduced her to breathing techniques to help her work on feeling calm, centred and in an attempt to switch from possible unconscious fight or flight mode to a more "neutral" mode of being, **Olivia practised her breathing daily**. Not only did she feel calmer in herself from 10 minutes of active conscious breathing each day, but she also in less than a week had stopped the uncontrollable sweats. Oliva thought and assumed that she had no worries or anxieties in her life and, when consulted, there didn't appear to be any major issues. She did report back that **the breathing shifted how she felt for the better** and the calmer feelings she experienced during and after the breathing practice left her feeling in many ways calmer than she had been for years. Actively making her mind and body shift to a calmer space while breathing helped her physical symptoms, which she no longer experienced. For Olivia it was simply about giving herself a short amount of time to breathe, which allowed her to feel the very many benefits physically as well as mentally and to create a sense of inner peace and control.

Peter was never present. His mind raced ahead to the next day, the next week, the next deal, the next project, the next anything that began to leave him experiencing anxiety. As one area of his life would close and complete, he would naturally wander off to the next. He wanted to feel more present, as he felt he was always physically on edge too. Taking my advice, he began to practise daily mindfulness by **using his sense of sight, sound and from what he could physically feel through**

his awareness of his present time and space. He would often **interrupt his pattern of overthinking by pausing the mental movies and moving them out to the distance**, then actively bringing his mind into the present space and place of his physical body. For Peter, he felt he had discovered a way that he could divert his mind to the present moment, which left him feeling mentally and physically at ease quite quickly. As he would often say, "Small changes can and do lead to big differences."

In all of these examples, each individual paid attention to their specific issue, their way of thinking, and then utilized the Anxiety Antidote methods to improve their mental and physical state for the better. It required practice, patience and perseverance on a daily basis to override the old anxious patterns that were not positively serving them in their life. This was all achieved through accountability. It will only take you a small amount of time each day to activate the desired methods that you need so that you can also develop improved ways of thinking that help you think, feel and live better.

Consider for yourself:

- Could you spare two minutes to practise feeling present?
- Do you have time to actively take 15 slow, deep, calming, relaxing breaths?
- Have you got the time to interrupt your thought patterns to create an immediate effect on stopping the pathways of anxious thinking that often pull you deeper into the feelings of anxiety?

It all comes down to the choices that you make to work on your thoughts and most importantly the cause of your anxiety. The cause could be your irrational thoughts that continually spiral into possible situations that feed the feelings of anxiety into your body. The cause may well be something specific in your life that you need to actively work on, change, stop or improve, which may then bring a natural ending to your anxious thoughts. In delaying working on the more physical cause in your life, the chance of your anxiety being prolonged and continuing into your day-to-day life will continue as you allow the power to remain in the situation to continue. Whether you choose physical action or mental action, your choices will lead you to relief as and when you choose to deal with your mind or your reality.

SCROLLING
THROUGH LIFE

The clock goes by, and the day moves on, and you are
distracted by each app, each timeline and every part of
the day where you detach from the present world. When
you're online, you do not feel your anxiety, and then you see
"him", "her", "they" and feel crap from where it's happening
online to where you are in your life. You do it over and
over. Day after day. But today you're making a choice to feel
something beyond this trance of time wasting. Remember,
you are the alchemist of your own potion of inner peace.

PART THREE

NEW SELF

Having explored your personal subjective experience through a variety of coaching questions to help you turn your focus within yourself, you may have got to a place of clarity in identifying and understanding the many components of your anxiety. The **self-action** methods will have given you the chance to experiment and work with your thoughts and may have led to a variety of changes and results. Your ability to feel, activate and experience your inner **GPS** may now, through practice and repetition, have become habitual. In many ways you may feel a new sense of "self" developing through actively putting the antidote into action within your day-to-day life. This self that you have given birth to is in many ways helping you to return to the factory settings of inner peace that were naturally there before your experiences led you to adopt anxious patterns. It is through the new that you can overpower the old. It is through the conscious actions of choices that you make to take your power where you can create the **new self** that you now desire.

AN EYE
TO THE FUTURE

As we have discovered, the key to your power is to take action on what you need to work on with your mind and emotions. But often it can be difficult putting this knowledge into practice – especially when help is required for ourselves, rather than others.

The only person that can move you into a position of thinking and feeling better is yourself, but there is a lot of help out there. You can follow the methods outlined in the book and work on yourself and your anxiety or you can seek professional help to have a practitioner help facilitate the changes you desire. Should you require one-to-one assistance, I have included a list of therapies at the end of this book (see page 215).

Without working on your mind and your thoughts, without changing and developing better ways of thinking, you may find yourself continually challenged by your anxiety.

Dealing with your thought patterns can be much easier than changing and working on the people, situations and causes of anxiety in your life. However, the choice to end, work on and work through your anxiety will always fundamentally be yours and will be determined by how you choose to use your time. By taking daily steps and regular action, you can develop your mind to have more positive and, eventually, habitual ways of thinking that help you with the rest of your life.

UPDATING YOUR MINDSET AND IDENTITY

The power now lies in your hands and in your mind as you move forward with your day-to-day life to create a new sense of self and update your mindset. It can be helpful to often consider for yourself:

- What action will I now take with my anxiety?
- How will I create the changes that I desire?
- What specific things do I need to do?

In any NLP coaching session, it is important for the individual who is exploring their life, their goals, outcomes and even areas of mindset to take accountability in creating the results that they desire. Any practitioner, therapist or coach simply facilitates the exploration, the map of the experience and then helps to define with the individual the best approach to use moving forward. It is the individual's actions, use of time, choices and therefore accountability outside and between sessions to put the work into action and then create the desired results. This can continue to be measured through follow-up sessions to then focus on their approach, realign and then re-strategize where necessary. How many blenders, coffee machines, books, even items of clothing have you purchased and not made effective use of? Getting value from the time and money that you invest in will always come down to your choices to make good use of the purchases that you make. In considering your own accountability you can ask yourself in relation to your anxiety and the exploration that you have experienced with working through the methods:

- What action will I now take with my anxiety?
- How will I create the changes that I desire?
- What specific things do I need to do?

In developing new ways of working with your mind and in exploring the relationship with your thoughts on a day-to-day basis where you may be feeling anxious, the most immediate consideration you may need is "**What can I do right now?**" **Awareness must lead to action**, especially if you have allowed your anxiety to exist, build, develop and grow over long periods of time without any action on finding inner peace. The Anxiety Antidote in action comes from you taking the right dose of what you need to do with your thoughts, to think and feel better to reduce or even eliminate your anxiety.

Through all of the positive and healthy ways that you attempt to work on and work with your anxiety, you are placing yourself in a position where you are aiming to take control over how you think and feel. Instead of being an observer who views and feels the experiences that your mind is formulating through your thoughts, you can in fact shift the gear to slow down, to take action, and to move yourself to a position of potential relief. Self-action can always lead to results. If you sit and watch your experience, if you allow the feelings to overwhelm you, you are in many ways allowing your anxiety to dominate the way that you feel and live. In using your awareness and in putting into practice the methods that you can use on yourself and for yourself, you can powerfully and quickly change and transform how you feel for the better. Any choice of the designated methods can help you to take the remote control of how you are thinking and therefore feeling, to intervene on the world that you are experiencing within. This point of self-power comes through you choosing to take control and then choosing to take action. It is in this position where you must shift your focus to "**What can I do right now?**" to help yourself feel better so that you can move from being a victim of your personal experience to becoming your own saviour.

It's generally a natural instinct to care for those in your life that require assistance. From the person who falls down in the street, the homeless person asking for change, to the individual who needs direction to their destination, there are moments where you will open your heart and unconditionally give. The ability to care for others will personally stretch further for those that are close to you. You may naturally care for your parents, your partner and your children if you have them. Your close circle of friends and family, however big or small, will always sit on your radar for those moments where you need to offer a helping hand. Care and assistance always comes from you opening your heart. It may feel as though you wouldn't question the need of others and always be open to assisting those that need help.

With anxiety, you are the person who is in need, and you are the person who has to help your own needs and also the needs of your anxiety. Any resistance in helping yourself can only prolong your own pain and suffering.

Think back to any past young toddler whether more recent or from a long time ago that you can now think of. A toddler will communicate the best way it knows how, perhaps the only way it knows how, through noise. Unable to speak or verbalize sentences or even the right singular words, the sounds and expressions will always be a call to get an adult's attention. In an uncomfortable emotional state, the noise of the toddler will get louder. Their call and needs will become more persistent and it's natural to care and offer immediate support to the toddler that is there and in need. In most cases you may not know what their **needs** or **wants** are, yet they continue to communicate the best way they know, and it's almost certain that you would offer care and assistance over ignoring or neglecting the young toddler. Would you leave the toddler for a day, weeks, months or years calling out in need?

Would you leave your anxiety for a day, weeks, months, or years calling out in need?

- What action will I now take with my anxiety?
- How will I create the changes that I desire?
- What specific things do I need to do?

If you keep doing what you're doing, you're going to have the same experiences and results in your life. Wandering the roads ahead of "what ifs" as you think through all of the possible difficulties you may one day face is only going to feed the feelings of anxiety and in fact train your mind to re-engage in this route of anxious thinking automatically. The more that you entertain this anxious way of thinking, the more habitual it will become for your thoughts to naturally transport you into a future place of thinking through anxiety. Feeling fear in the present moment doesn't have to be your reality. Walking the cliff edge of what might one day happen in your mind doesn't need to have you living life on the edge. The choice of being mindful and actively encouraging yourself to break the cycle, to interrupt the patterns of thinking that disturb you can and will allow you to form better thinking habits that will become your new normal over time. Resetting your current mind settings that have been born from life experiences, which leave you to think, feel and exist in anxious ways is the journey you can now go on, utilizing the many "**self-action**" ways demonstrated to you to work with and on your anxiety. Realize the importance of mopping up, sorting out, decluttering and re-wiring the old, unhelpful, broken and possible destructive ways of thinking that have continued to feed your anxious mind and body. Restoring order within to cancel out any "dis-order" that you may feel can and will come from you working with and developing a new relationship with your mind.

This relationship starts with you firstly becoming aware of your thoughts, to then interrupt, change, develop and reset the operating system of your mind that is in place. Allow yourself patience and continue to practise the necessary steps, methods and procedures as you give time to your mind and emotions. Whether you tidy your house, attend to your garden or spend time learning how to work and operate your phone, allow yourself time, discipline and commitment to now **developing a new relationship with your mind**. This will help you to navigate through your anxious thoughts internally and help you transform your experiences externally as you begin to expand the map and model of your own personal world. Any new journey takes time, focus and clear thinking so that it can become unconsciously normal to travel to the desired place without thinking. In allowing yourself to walk slowly, regularly and frequently along these new pathways of thinking, you can transform your current ways of being, to quickly becoming old unhelpful patterns that simply serve you no positive purpose in your life.

PUT YOUR OXYGEN
MASK ON FIRST

If you breathe into your body, a force of energy flows through you that allows you to exist. As you breathe into your body, you allow the channels that regulate your being to return to their preferred settings.

To heal yourself, you need to understand yourself and, in your new learnings, you will have come to learn that the power lies within the choices you make in your mind, with your thoughts, to end your own suffering.

COACHING
YOURSELF

As you begin to actively work on yourself, there may be times where you feel challenged, deflated and demotivated. It's usually in these times where it is necessary for you to keep moving forward with the work that you are doing, as significant breakthroughs can then be achieved. To help you stay focused, on track with your personal development journey and to increase a sense of self-motivation when required, I want you to consider in great detail how you really want your life to be without anxiety. You will have considered to some degree this reality at the very start of the book. Having now understood the very many aspects of your mind for how you formulate your thoughts, the patterns of anxiety that may relate to you, and having experienced various positive shifts through the self-action methods, you may now think and feel quite differently with regards to your anxiety. There can often be a shift, where you now feel more resourceful and, in many ways, more powerful. Whether you're feeling strong or inspired, motivated or still discovering how to work with your anxiety, you may well create a new or updated personal outcome from the questions that follow.

Spend some time considering the following:

1. What will your life look like when you are living in ways where your anxiety is manageable, or not even present?

2. What will you hear when you are in this space and place in your life? Think about your inner voice. What will it be saying? Also consider how the spaces around you will sound when you're in this better space.

3. How will you feel without the feelings of anxiety?

4. What will this then allow you to do in your life?

5. Who will it allow you to be?

6. Will this freedom that you experience influence other people in your life?

7. What aspects of your life will feel a positive difference?

8. When do you want to have these results?

Spend some time really thinking about each question and allow yourself to see what you see, hear what you hear, and feel what you feel as you shift your thinking from where you are to where you really and truly want to be in your life.

MAKE AN ACTION PLAN

Now that you have thought through and considered what you want your life to look like, free from your anxiety, the most important question for you to now consider is:

What action do you specifically need to take from this very day to make your goal your reality?

Write out the steps and the actions that come to mind that will help you to formulate a plan to move forward in achieving your outcome. For each step or action you've written, ask yourself:

How is this going to help me moving forward?

Allow yourself time to inhabit the future in your thoughts and notice how it makes you feel. Think ahead through your answers, see it in your mind and feel this desired future outcome in your body.

Now ask yourself: **If I *don't* take action, what results will I get?**

Consider the consequences that you may face from not working on the steps required to move you from where you are to where you want to be.

Notice your answers and think about what you really need to do – how you need to act, think and manage your time – to really create the changes that you desire in your life.

Visualizing your outcome, to hear that space and place where you do want to be, and to connect to the feelings that you will feel from achieving that reality, will help you to stay motivated and focused. You only have to see your outcome in your mind to feel the feelings in your body, and that visual reminder can help you to move closer to the space and place that you do want to be in your life.

FEEL FREE

Hope is the key that unlocks you from the bounds of anxiety.

The lane that you drive down with the direction of your thoughts will lead you to areas of darkness or openings of light. A closed mind of "what ifs" powerfully tightens the door to mental and emotional freedom. A consciousness of ease comes from being mindful of where you go with your thoughts that then leads you to feel on edge or at peace. Think about how you want to feel.

Choose hope to open your mind and to free your body, as one powerful hopeful thought can overpower the feelings within and shift you to calmer waters, within your emotional body.

Feel hopeful by experiencing hope in your mind. Spend time in hope's arms and be rocked into a blissful space and place of living, by choosing the direction of your thoughts.

Hope is the key.

CHANGING YOUR VIEW

Having helped you consult, explore and search within the space and place of your thoughts – which has allowed you to identify your feelings and the cause of those feelings, and understand the type of thinker that you are – and provided you with the methods and interventions that can help you find mental and emotional ease, the power now lies in you developing a new relationship with your mind. This section is in some ways similar to the kind of conversation I would have with a client having gone through a number of sessions from start to finish, highlighting the importance that they follow the plan of action that is prescribed. I want to now highlight that you now have in your hands the many questions that will help you to turn your focus within, an outline of the patterns and symptoms that will help you relate and understand to your anxiety, and most importantly the methods and processes to use, as and when needed, to allow you to create the antidote to your anxiety.

Through awareness, time, self-action and repetition, you have the opportunities and power to become the antidote to your own personal anxiety experience.

In a fast-moving world where deliveries can arrive on the same day that you place your order, it can often feel frustrating when you don't see results. Weight loss and muscle building is a gradual process. Decorating a room requires preparation and time, and learning how to drive requires a great deal of learning and practice. Now you are beginning your daily practice of working with your mind and your thoughts to bring ease to your feelings of anxiety, it is important that you practise and remain persistent in utilizing your new skills. The chance to use any of the suggested methods will come from your day-to-day experiences that lead your mind to create your anxiety. If you're engaging in anxious thinking about situations that are present in your life, there's no doubt that the feelings of anxiety will be keeping you company in your life. The key is to deal with your thoughts and anxious feelings as and when you experience them. In dealing with things when they happen, or in cancelling out the thought patterns that build the feelings of anxiety, you can rapidly bring yourself to a place of more mental and emotional ease. This comes from you choosing to act on the way that you're thinking so that you can transform how you're feeling, as you intervene to end the anxiety that could be building within.

Personally and professionally, people tell me about ongoing situations in their lives that cause them to feel anxious. This can be with their careers and people involved in them, family situations, relationship challenges or even with aspects of their health. The solution that will bring an end to their anxiety lies in the choices and actions they could take. For a lot of people, their anxiety is being prolonged because the individual is not stepping in to deal with the cause. Dealing with that person or situation at work, communicating or setting boundaries in a challenged relationship, or resolving family situations could help these people end their anxiety. These situations, and there may be some similar ones in your own life, require more than just interventions to the mind and the way that you are thinking; they may require action that involves other people or actual work on the situations in hand.

When is a good time to end the situation, or to address it or to work things through in relation to the cause of your own personal anxiety? It all comes down to the choices that you are making and in terms of the anxiety that you experience. You may have found yourself avoiding dealing with the root cause of your anxiety or even allowing the situation that causes you to experience anxiety to still be a part of your life. This can cause you to have an underlying constant feeling of being on edge, living at times in fear and experience generalized anxiety.

MENTAL BOUNDARIES

Should you find yourself in a situation that is prolonged in your life that can't be dealt with immediately as there are other people involved, you can then work on your focus and the train of your thoughts. In setting mental boundaries for yourself so that you do not carry the situation into your evening, after work, during social situations, or in any other times where you cannot at that time deal with the situation that's causing anxiety, you should action boundaries to mentally have free time and space within your thoughts to not be overly consumed by your anxious thoughts. This can be achieved by you using your awareness, the self-action methods, and by actively managing your thoughts for the better. Managing your thoughts is one option and "scheduling" time to be anxious, to think things through, to let the thoughts be expressed and felt, to allow yourself the time and space for the feelings and thoughts to surface, can also be considered. This can be helpful in managing your mind and your anxious thoughts so that you actively choose to have them when you allow them, so that they are not always at the forefront of your mind.

HOW LONG WILL IT TAKE?

One of the most common questions that I get asked is "How long will it take me to improve my anxiety?" and my answer is always the same: anxiety is subjective and individual to each person. It needs to be understood, explored for how it is formed and constructed in the mind, and then the area of the person's life needs to be considered for the cause of the anxiety, or interventions on the thought patterns need to be actioned to find relief.

Any of the work suggested throughout this book is work in progress. You can practise the methods suggested, measure the changes that you experience and begin to develop better thought patterns that serve you in more positive ways. If you do find that your anxiety is still surfacing, then consider some one-to-one assistance as it may be that you require a deeper and more personal intervention.

YOUR PERSONAL GPS - MAGIC

Look around, see the stillness, hear the calm and feel at one with your present space. See, hear and feel.

PREPARE TO LAND

Within every great challenge lies a variety of potential opportunities that can be birthed into your growing reality. Even if they start in your mind as a concept, a conversation or a movie of what you think of within. It is there. Start the mind show and have that internal conversation, because you know what to do and how to change things; you are just riding the same train that you know all too well. Walk more. Run. Sail into the sunset of your dreams because the magic of the world is waiting for you to hug you and to remind you that life on the edge is only a concept of your mind and imagination. Free yourself to be, to feel, live and go. You are here for magic and there's so much more to be had, shared and experienced, if you can allow yourself to freely think beyond the current full stop that has paused your story.

FURTHER RESOURCES

Some professional services that I recommend you consider and research should you require one-to-one assistance with your anxiety include:

NEURO-LINGUISTIC PROGRAMMING (NLP)

The study of your subjective anxiety experience can allow you to get a deeper understanding with a skilled practitioner of the mental strategies that run and action your anxiety. In working on the thought patterns to reduce and intervene on the current mental strategies to then install positive tools and techniques that help you to feel less anxious, a more personal approach may help you find relief. Working on ending any inner conflict where you may require "parts integration", emotional anchors being collapsed and in expanding your filters of deletion, distortion and generalization where required, you may find that over a course of sessions you experience small changes that lead to big differences in your life. It is also through a skilled practitioner where you may get deeper clarity over whether you need to work on your mindset or the situations and circumstances in your life. From analysing your personal situation and from exploring your individual map of your world in a more personal manner, you may well find faster results.

INTEGRAL EYE MOVEMENT THERAPY (IEMT)

A skilled IEMT practitioner can help relieve anxiety triggers and the feelings they elicit. Any past flashbacks or difficult experiences which may be unconsciously activating present anxiety can be bought to the surface through specific questioning to help use the process of IEMT to then collapse and desensitize the anxiety trigger. This advanced and rapid process can help bring overwhelming feelings and memories to collapse in their strength, which can have immediate and long-term changes on anxiety.

HYPNOSIS

Working with the unconscious mind to facilitate change and understanding on a deeper level of consciousness where anxiety may be operating and influencing from a younger age. Suggestion therapy to "restore" a sense of calm, ease and a sense of relaxation can not only help the mind recentre away from past anxious experiences, but it can help relax the mind and body on a deeper level. The actual process of a hypnosis induction, and full session from a skilled practitioner, can help relax the individual to then help shift from fight or flight mode. Helping the person relax and achieve a deeper sense of calm within can in many ways help the individual before the suggestion or regression work takes place. A number of sessions can then help have a long-term impact on deepening the individual's ability to relax, leaving them feeling the benefits of the process. Regressing back to specific significant memories or experiences can also help with open communication to the unconscious mind, which helps the present-day self stop "operating" from this past way of thinking and feeling. Working on a deeper unconscious level, to offer suggestions, and even automatic post-hypnotic suggestions to help the person's unconscious assist them to reduce their anxiety, can help in many ways to bring the anxiety to ease.

MINDFULNESS

From breathing techniques and journaling to mindful activities that encourage you to have focus, discipline and a deeper awareness of the present space and place that you exist in, mindfulness can help you shift your focus from anxious thinking. Fully engaging in the moment to whatever degree of focus you can achieve can help you in many ways to train your thoughts to be less anxious. The ability to be focused and to increase your mind's attention span can also help you actively and more consciously shift your awareness from anything that's not serving you positively to then feel the ease more presently in your mind and body. Awareness is always powerful for how the mind works and how to change and interrupt the patterns of thinking that cause you emotional stress. Awareness of the present moment is golden if you can find the ability to shift and flow into it as and when desired.

ABOUT THE AUTHOR

Kamran Bedi is a mental health and wellbeing practitioner who utilizes Neuro Linguistic Programming, Hypnosis, Mindfulness and Integral Eye Movement Therapy in his coaching sessions. He works with various people from the media, CEO's, school teachers and nurses and also offers wellbeing workshops around mindset to various universities and performing arts institutions.

As a certified trainer of NLP and Hypnosis, Kamran also offers training and certification to master practitioner level. It is through his courses where he gets to further explore the skills and methods of NLP and Hypnosis with his course students, which allows his experience and research around this field to continue to grow. He is passionate about educating people about how to be mindful, how to understand the 'structure and set-up' of their mind and how to develop a better relationship with their thoughts in relation to the past and future.

He has worked in the field of self-development since 2008 and is continually learning and developing his professional skills as well as his own personal development.

kamranbedi.com
mindbodymethod.co.uk
@coachkamranbedi

ACKNOWLEDGMENTS

Writing this book has been an enjoyable journey where I have had encouraging guidance from Lucy Carroll across the whole process, and the entire Watkins publishing team, thank you.

I would like to extend my gratitude to Emma Mumford for introducing me to Watkins and for her endless support. A special thanks to David for his love and encouragement and to Kelly Hoppen, Arlene Phillips, and Katie Piper for expressing their support for my work.

I am eternally grateful to Narinder, Gurdip, Nicky, Gurcharan and the entire 'clan', for I would be nothing without your endless sacrifices that are so influential for all that I achieve and experience personally and professionally.

Thanks to everyone who I have had the pleasure of working with as clients in 1-1 sessions, group workshop members and students who take my practitioner courses, my learning from your time and energy has allowed me to understand the many ways of personal development and transformation.